D1196171

# NOVEMBER'S GLADIATORS

# NOVEMBER'S GLADIATORS

*Inside Stories of White House Advancemen,
the Road Warriors of Presidential Campaigns*

# TERRY BAXTER

Langdon Street Press
Minneapolis, MN

Langdon Street Press
322 First Avenue N, 5th floor
Minneapolis, MN 55401
612.455.2293
www.langdonstreetpress.com

ISBN-13: 978-1-62652-630-3
LCCN: 2014900502

Distributed by Itasca Books

Cover photo courtesy of the Reagan Library
photo by Patricia Sadtler Baxter

Cover Design and Typeset by Sophie Chi

*Printed in the United States of America*

To Fair Patricia
Ashley & Bryan
And to all the wonderful small-town Americans
who helped us spread our temporary canvas to
bring the political circus

Also by Terry Baxter

*Hailstone*

*The Ursa Ultimatum*

# Contents

# PROLOGUE

You are a presidential advanceman. You arrive in a small town with only a single person's phone number: the local party chairman. You have few local resources, but you have a mission. And, you have one amazing bionic superpower: you are the personal representative of the President of the United States. In only a few days, you will plan and execute a presidential visit that will electrify the entire town. You will marshal the press, you will attract the crowds, and you will provide the color and atmosphere people will talk about long after the music has faded.

If you are good, you will amass a score of devoted volunteers and lead them to accomplish feats they would have said were impossible. If you are *really* good, they will think they did it themselves. Many of them will correspond with you for years to come.

Humans are social animals. Being part of an exclusive team is a powerful elixir. As an advanceman, you especially enjoy being an alpha member of the pack. You may work for the White House, or you may be a volunteer yourself, the product of a rigorous selection process that lands you in the rarified air of a presidential campaign. Twenty-hour days follow twenty-hour days. There are no weekends, no holidays, only week after week of endless challenges. But there are extraordinary rewards—colleagues you will never forget, townspeople who became lifelong friends in the heat of battle, and the personal satisfaction of meeting the test. And, if you are very lucky, the election of a candidate you admire and trust to do the best job for America.

I was privileged to be in the company of these men and women. So, what makes a rational, accomplished candidate run for President of the United States, where they will face an unrelenting gauntlet of character assassination, knee-jerk disdain for their policy proposals, and the physical and mental exhaustion of the campaign? Like human nature, the motivations are complex, impossible to pigeonhole, and, for the survivors of the process, unquenchable. The reasons range from high-minded to venal, from patriotism and political conviction to ambition and lust for power.

To paraphrase Felix Rohatyn, who is often called the "last old wise man on Wall Street," when he was struggling to save New York City from bankruptcy in the 1970s, "The greatest tragedy is when a man could make a difference, but doesn't join the fight." I was fortunate to mostly work for candidates who chose to make a difference.

At our first advance seminar, I asked my fellow advancemen-to-be why they were volunteering for the campaign. A few answers were insipid, the equivalent of "I like to work with people" in a job interview. A number were just frivolous: "I want to carry the awesome credentials"; "I want to rub shoulders with the movers and shakers"; "I want to access the corridors of power." Only a few were thoughtful, mostly along the lines of "I truly believe in the candidate" or "I want to contribute to the political process." What we all shared was a nearly visible reservoir of energy that radiated from our pores. I had never recognized that in myself, but it must have been detectable to those who selected us.

Over the course of the campaign we would travel to every corner of America, and after the election, the world. We would become catalysts in the electoral outcome and witness history. We would become: ADVANCEMEN.

*　*　*

In the fall of election years, the bars of every battleground state are filled with eager, young political operatives. Often both presidential candidates are advancing the same town, so we mingle freely in the bars. We have no animosity; we are kindred spirits. We swap tales and buy each other drinks.

Advancemen are the road warriors of the campaigns, the fighter jocks, the top guns. *Every* volunteer thinks of himself as an advanceman. The newcomers who line up the motorcades call themselves advancemen; the sign makers and crowd checkers call themselves advancemen; even the young intern who holds the sign identifying the restrooms calls himself an advanceman. But the *real* advancemen are a small cadre moving from town to town to direct each candidate's visit, organize the volunteers, and position the post-standers. They direct security, communications, the media arrangements, and all the myriad details of the event. They help the local community prepare for a presidential visit or enjoy a political rally. I would bestow the title advanceman on a talented few—the Secret Service lead, the staff lead, the press advance, and a couple of site directors. *These* are the guys who walk with a swagger and have tales to tell.

In forty years of business and government experience, I have never met a more able group. The men and women who have climbed the ladder from press advance, motorcade advance, hotel advance, or site advance to become lead staff advanceman for the White House are unparalleled leaders, planners, directors, and decision makers—add "diplomats" under intense pressure to deal with constant change and come up with the optimum solution. We have often told ourselves: if the government consisted of a hundred advancemen, Washington would actually work.

Advancemen have shared historic public moments and intimate private moments. They have enjoyed the exhilaration of a perfect campaign stop, and suffered fiascos that disintegrated into chaos.

After three campaigns, three inaugurations, and a half-dozen foreign trips, these are my memories of some of those moments.

# MISS APRIL

I was thirty-nine years old, near death by advancemen standards. This was my first event of the 1984 Reagan campaign, a Las Vegas fundraiser. Another old-timer, Walt McCay, was the lead advance—he was pushing fifty. All the rest of the team members were whippersnappers. Perhaps my age had qualified me for the night's escapade, but to this day I suspect it was my retreating hairline that induced Walt to select me for his secret mission.

Walt McCay had assigned me to the hotel where the presidential party would overnight. Now, I was standing in the hallway outside a room where Walt assured me the most important part of my duties awaited. The door was cracked an inch, so I knocked and cautiously said, "Hello . . ."

Thirty minutes before, Walt and the rest of the team had accompanied the elaborately assembled presidential motorcade to the airport, where they would orchestrate the presidential arrival ceremony. After a brief press availability, Walt and the presidential party would caravan to the hotel, where I was entrusted with the arrangements in the president's suite.

President Reagan's schedule said, "private time," but it was an open secret he would be greeted with an impromptu celebration of his seventy-third birthday. Twenty carefully screened guests were assembled in the suite: the hotel manager, a bevy of political heavyweights, several friends from the area, and a select group of big shots from the next day's fundraiser. The hotel had produced a giant cake in the shape of the White House, and champagne was cooling.

Preparations complete, I had sprinted to the more public end of the hotel to finish my last detail: collecting Walt's date. This was Walt's vital secret mission for me.

There was a hint of steam from the crack in the door, but no answer to my knock. I pushed the door open six more inches and again called, "Hello . . ."

"Come in Darlin'," said a cheerful feminine voice.

I steeled myself. Sherrie. Miss April, by rumor. As Walt's personal guest, she had been invited to meet the president, and therefore had been cleared by the Secret Service with the same diligence as all the other guests, but the underground gossip newswire had reported that she was a gorgeous centerfold. I entered the room and closed the door. Immediately on my right was an open bathroom door, where standing in a faint mist from the shower was Miss April. She had a towel wrapped around her hair, but was otherwise completely naked. She smiled sweetly.

Did I say completely naked?

I had done a lengthy stint on the Ford campaign in 1976. I worked on the inauguration after President Reagan's first election. I held a responsible executive position in a major company, and I'd had a normal range of worldly experiences, but standing face to face with a naked centerfold was somehow missing from my skill set. My face colored embarrassingly.

She was totally unfazed by my presence. "Oh Hon', don't be cross with me. I can be ready in two shakes." She accented the "two shakes" with a quick sashay of her hips. The Secret Service gossip was confirmed: she was gorgeous.

"We have to hurry," I said cleverly. I thought my voice was remarkably steady. Perhaps not.

"Just help me zip this up." She pulled the dress on over her head. No bra, no panties. Although my focus may have wavered, I zipped professionally. She tossed the towel and fluffed her hair. "See, I told you I could be quick." The dress deliciously followed her curves, but was modest, and well, classy. Sherrie was sensational. She gave me a peck on the cheek just before applying her lipstick.

While she stepped into her high heels, my earpiece announced, "All cars and stations, signal arrive, signal arrive." Air Force One had landed.

Almost immediately Walt radioed me, "Baxter, Baxter, McCay."

I responded with our radio protocol, "McCay, Baxter."

"Baxter, go November." This instruction was a request for me to switch my White House radio from the main frequency, Sierra, to the back-up frequency, November. There were two usual reasons for this: first, a lengthy conversation, which might otherwise tie up the Sierra channel unnecessarily, or second, the caller wanted to speak more privately. Of course, both frequencies were "in the open," or party-line frequencies. So, in practice, curiosity often impelled the entire net to switch over to November to eavesdrop on the "secret" conversation.

I switched the frequency, imagining every Secret Service agent doing the same. "McCay, Baxter. Go ahead."

"Terry, we are loading up. Is the package in place?"

"The wrapping is finally finished," I said.

She giggled.

"Two minutes."

"Great. Coming your way."

Sherrie took my arm and we strode purposely to the secure end of the hotel. The agents at each checkpoint gave me knowing smiles as we just marched on like two prom dates.

I was sure the color was still high on my cheeks as we entered the suite, but none of the milling guests seemed to notice. I got their attention and told them the president was on his way. We rehearsed the program again. When the president entered, everyone would sing "Happy Birthday." Then the president would go around the semi-circle of guests so the photographer could shoot individual pictures. I had collected all the names and addresses. Once the photos were inscribed ("Thank you for your assistance and support, Ronald Reagan"), I would send them out a week or two later.

The president would cut the cake. Each guest would get a piece from the steward. Five champagne minutes later, I would escort all of the guests out so the president could enjoy "private time" after his long day.

My earpiece updates finally indicated "one minute out," so I arranged the guests in the order of my checklist, placing Miss April midway along the row of photo subjects. I made a gesture for quiet with a finger to my lips. We were ready to "surprise" the president. Walt came in first. After a brief survey of the room, he gave me a satisfied glance. Miss April squared her shoulders to magnificent effect. The president entered with a big smile. The guests yelled, "Happy birthday," and began to sing.

The president, as always, was genial. He pretended to be surprised by the huge cake. He beamed for each photo, but did seem particularly animated when he greeted Miss April. After the pictures, the guests circulated, trying not to obviously cluster around the president. They mostly failed.

Walt and Sherrie reconnected over champagne and birthday cake. I distinctly heard her whisper, "He was just a hoot, I was naked as a jay bird . . ." To my relief, they both laughed. They left the suite with the other guests, hand-in-hand. At the end of the hall, she looked back over her shoulder and gave me a little wave.

I never saw Sherrie again, but even twenty-nine years later, my mental image is indelible. How, you might ask, did I snag the job of escorting Miss April to the president's birthday party? Well, it was mainly a brief dose of hubris, which led me in a direction I never expected. It was all thanks to a gag writer. . . .

# The Halls of the White House

In 1976, I was the director of communications for GEICO in the Washington suburb of Chevy Chase. I managed the employee communications as well as training and development. I was a Republican, but not politically active.

I joined GEICO in 1972 after five years of racing cars full time. When our son was born, my mother told me racing was no career for someone with a family. "Why don't you get a real job like all the other kids?" she nagged. I couldn't dispute her logic. "Mom," I told her proudly, "I have joined a rock-solid industry, insurance."

Over the next several years, GEICO proceeded to ruin forty years of sterling history through mismanagement, bad choices, and a sinking economy. By 1976, GEICO was on the brink of insolvency (the insurance term for bankruptcy). The company was about to become the biggest hole in the ground in the history of the insurance industry.

So much for motherly advice.

In the darkest hour, the GEICO board fired the chairman and president and hired Jack Byrne, a distinguished former

Travelers executive, to save the company. For the first months, Byrne was a mystery man to the GEICO employees. We watched lines of limos arrive outside the company while he wrestled with regulators, banking officials, and accountants to try to rescue GEICO. We read in the evening papers that GEICO was sure to fail. My wife and I had just bought a new house, and, nervous that we'd be forced to move right out again, left most of the furniture stacked in the garage. Good employees started to drift away from the company.

One morning I stood outside Byrne's office at 6:00 a.m. when he was rumored to arrive. "Who are you?" he asked.

"I'm in charge of employee communications, and employees need to hear from you. We are getting all of our information, what little there is, from *The Washington Post*, and your best employees are starting to bail out. You'll have no one left but the drones unless you talk to them yourself."

He glared at me with a bulldog expression, and then motioned, "Okay, come in."

He spent three hours with me until I had run out of questions. His secretary kept trying to interrupt, but he waved her off. I did a special edition of the employee newspaper with Byrne's vision for GEICO's future and the steps required to make it happen. I can't say that it stemmed the tide of departures, but perhaps it helped.

A week later, when Byrne needed feedback on a financial presentation to New York insurance analysts, he called for me to join the vice president of investor relations and the vice president of marketing to listen to his rehearsal in the board room. I had never been in the board room before. This was heady company. The three of us listened to Byrne's hour and twenty-minute talk.

"Well, what do you think?" he asked.

"Jack," the hale-fellow-well-met investor relations manager said familiarly, "you'll knock 'em dead."

My heart sank. I didn't agree. The marketing director remained silent.

I swallowed hard. This could be my last day at GEICO, but he had asked for my opinion. "It was terrible," I said.

His eyebrows shot up. "Really?" he said leaning forward. "Why?"

"Well," I considered hedging, but decided to go all in. "It was too long. At lunchtime, they'll only listen for twenty or thirty minutes. Most of your remarks were just boilerplate from the annual report, they should already know all of that. And there was only about two minutes that you seemed to have any real passion for . . ."

"What two minutes?" Byrne demanded.

I flipped through the script and pointed, "This part here."

He lurched forward like he might strike me and said, "Do you know *that* two minutes is the only part of this whole pile of crap I wrote myself?"

No, I didn't know, but I felt as if a little sunbeam had just fallen on me. Byrne gestured to the two other men, "Thanks fellows." He stood and said to me, "Come upstairs, we are going to rewrite this useless mess."

The presentation was a success. After many additional steps, the company was rescued, and in a year and a half, GEICO returned to profitability. But that is a different story.

Just before my first encounter with Jack Byrne, I read in *The Washington Post* that the White House speechwriters were going on strike because Gerald Ford had hired a gag writer, Don Penny, to spice up his remarks. According to the *Post*, this was an insult to the speechwriters' sensibilities, and no doubt their egos.

President Ford was presumably speechless.

After letting this information ferment for a short while, I came to the conclusion that *I* was the perfect humble hero to come to the rescue of President Ford. In a circuitous way, I knew Ford's appointments secretary, Terry O'Donnell (O'Donnell had married the lovely sister of my best man, John Kidder. We had occasionally shared a sofa and beer in front of Redskins games). I took the chance that he would remember my name, and left a message with the White House operator.

I was enormously impressed that he called me back (and I should say grateful for all that has followed). I explained that GEICO was in the nearby suburbs where I wrote speeches every day for the chairman of the board. I magnanimously volunteered to temporarily fill the void in the speechwriting staff.

O'Donnell laughed at *The Washington Post*'s story. "Never believe what you read in the press. Nobody is going on strike," he said. "The speechwriters are only a little disgruntled."

As I absorbed my disappointment, he continued, "But you've done television work, right?"

"Yes," I said, surprised that he even remembered my time at WETA and PBS.

"Well, I might have an even better place for you to volunteer your time. We are just about to have a huge celebration for the bicentennial of the United States, a sort of Fourth of July party on steroids. Great events: a parade of tall ships in New York Harbor, a special performance at the Kennedy Center, a ceremony at the National Archives to honor the Declaration of Independence, and we'll need an army of advancemen to handle the president's participation as well as the press. Your understanding of television requirements make you a natural."

In a matter of days I was checking in through the northwest gate of the White House for a meeting with Doug Blaser, the director of press advance. I tried not to show the goosebumps I was feeling as I walked through the corridors of the White House and the Old Executive Office Building (EOB).

Blaser was a take-charge, executive type—friendly in a brisk way, and nice, but all business. No small talk. He obviously considered my volunteering as a fait accompli. Apparently my referral from Terry O'Donnell was the only endorsement required. Blaser introduced me to some of the full-time press advancemen: Dorrance Smith, Steve Studdert, Dave Frederickson, David Wendell, and Jack Lacovey, each impressive and welcoming in his own way. Then he described the job. The lead press advanceman for a presidential event was expected to coordinate all of the arrangements for the press covering the event—press platforms, connections to the sound system, television-quality lighting, network feed lines, local press accreditation, transportation for the traveling press, appropriate releases to alert local media outlets, and, where necessary, press filing centers and office space for the White House press secretary (Ron Nessen, our ultimate boss) and other traveling staff.

Once an event began and the main elements of the press had reached their positions in the press pen or the press platform, the principal duty was to escort the press pool. The press pool was a small group, ten to fifteen, selected on a rotating basis to closely accompany the president. A network provided a camera crew. The AP and UPI wire photographers were included, along with several senior correspondents and a radio reporter. In a presidential motorcade, the pool traveled in specially equipped cars closely behind the presidential limo while all the rest of the press was transported in the press bus at the tail end.

In exchange for exclusive access to the president, the video, audio, photos, and reporting from the pool was immediately available to all the press. The pool reporters called their assignment "the death watch," presuming they were expected to record for history any sudden or dramatic development while the president was behind the scenes or transiting back hallways. The pool was also a space-saving and logistical device. When a portion of an event was not conducive to a thundering herd of television crews, the schedule would state, "pool coverage only." The saving grace of this strategy was that footage would be available to all.

The key for the lead press advanceman was to become intimately familiar with the president's movements and plan the pool movement to avoid interference while still maintaining close contact. This often involved dashes down backstage corridors, cordoned-off "pool chutes," and heads-down crouches around the presidential podium.

The White House press advance full-timers had killer credentials that they carried around in special cases. They were referred to as "commission books." I immediately coveted one. It was a flip-open case similar to FBI identification. The top half was a light blue etching of the White House overprinted with "White House Press Advance Representative." The bottom half included a gold-embossed seal of the President of the United States along with words and signatures encouraging access and cooperation.

I have to say my adrenaline was pumping as I savored the opportunity to be part of all this. I embarked on a series of "in-town" events, presidential appearances in Washington that involved the pool, to get familiar with the procedures—events I could do in the evenings or on long lunch breaks. The assignments were universally thrilling: collecting the pool from the West Wing press room, leading the press out through the Rose Garden to the South Lawn, riding in the presidential motorcade while tourists gawked and waved, and entering the back rooms and inner sanctums of official Washington.

By today's standards, personal communications were crude when I began doing advance work—no cell phones, PDAs, or instant e-mails. For consumers, touch-tone phones had only slowly replaced the venerable rotary dial over the prior ten years. Advance teams for the White House were supplied with two-way radios we called "bricks."

The Motorola radios were engineered by WHCA (pronounced wahcah), the White House communications agency, and were indeed about the size of bricks. Clipped on our belts, with a wire running down our suit sleeves ending in a small mike with a push-to-talk button nestled in our palms, we famously were said to be talking to our thumbs. Another wire sprouted from our collar, which ended in an earpiece. Most observers concluded we were Secret Service agents, who were similarly equipped. There were times, usually in bars, where we did little to dispel this impression.

The bricks connected us with other members of the advance team and the Secret Service, and by way of "signal" (the Army Signal Corps base station for the area of our trip) to a direct line in the White House, Air Force One, or any private telephone— an amazing capability for the time.

I got my own "pool pass," a laminated card that hung around my neck. It had an engraved image of the White House with "pool" printed across the bottom. One day, on the way out of GEICO, one of my colleagues said, "Wow, is that really a pass to the White House pool?" I nodded modestly. I didn't tell him it was the press pool, not the swimming pool.

We did several trips to the Republican National Headquarters, once for a speech, once for a dinner. On my first day I learned that Helen Thomas liked to edge her way out of the press pen in her own little game of hide and seek. Perhaps she thought she would uncover an exclusive from the receptionist at the RNC. I was naïve enough to think the press would observe the press pool rules, but not for long.

For the first couple of assignments, I accompanied one of the full-time press advance staffers. But on the third event, I was sent out alone. Of course, I still had the White House lead to direct the president's movements, and the Secret Service for protection, but on the president's schedule, "press advance" listed "Terry Baxter." I felt a flush of pride.

The Advance Office called me every hour by radio to check my progress. "Everything's okay," I reported each time.

After that, they cut the cord. I could fly without a net. I was one of the team.

After a few weeks of pool movements, the press seemed to lose their suspicion of me and began talking to me like one of the guys. They often grumbled about the boredom of the pool coverage.

"I have a thousand hours of video of motorcades snaking through Washington traffic where nothing happens," said one cameraman. "I think I'll take tomorrow off. No one will notice if I file the motorcade video from last week."

One night I was eating with the pool press at The Capitol Hill Club for the "Good Guys Dinner," a group of Republican congressmen who got together for fun and food every six weeks. On that evening President Ford was spreading goodwill and offering some remarks. My dinner partners were the AP and UPI writers Dick Grual and Frank Cormier, ABC's Charlie Gibson, and a few others.

They told me the story of a pool reporter who had a birthday party planned at home, but got assigned to pool duty. He decided to play hooky from pool duty for one afternoon. The dinner table reporter solemnly related how the hapless pool reporter was home with his family when President Kennedy's motorcade passed through Dallas on November 22, 1963. His publication missed a first-hand account of the story of the century.

No one skips pool assignments anymore.

The story had the sound of a tale enhanced for dramatic impact, but they all nodded as if it was a legend they believed. No matter how dreary the "ride-alongs" were, they would take their responsibilities seriously.

I would too.

# BICENTENNIAL OF THE
# UNITED STATES

WASHINGTON, D.C.

JULY 1976

Finally it was time for a major event, and I was again relegated to tagging along with a full-timer. Steve Studdert was the first of many memorable characters I encountered over the years. The background I got on him from the underground newswire was that he had been the chief of police in a small Midwestern town. When Steve moved mountains so impressively on a presidential trip through his town, he had been scooped up for a position on the White House staff. Now he was considered one of the best full-time White House press advance leads.

He was barrel chested and cock sure. He was the master of every detail of an event. His eyes, partially obscured behind glasses, gave little away, but a careful search usually revealed a hint of wry humor. His aura of authority was so striking I wondered if I could ever match it.

Another tidbit from the underground newswire claimed that once, when Studdert had missed the motorcade while solving some problem, he had "credentialed" a citizen (he had flagged down a passing car by waving his White House pass and then convinced the driver to chase down the motorcade so he could rejoin). The nonplused driver received a presidential photo and an entertaining cocktail party story.

Our event was one of two mainstays of the bicentennial, the ceremony honoring the Declaration of Independence at the National Archives on July 2. The president, vice president, Speaker of the House, and chief justice of the Supreme Court would each participate in a tribute to our founding documents, drawn up on this date two hundred years ago, then sign a visitors log to be stored in a time capsule until the next centennial.

With me in tow, Steve Studdert was everywhere at once, tweaking rope lines, adjusting the angle of the presidential podium, or testing the sound system feedback. When Steve was satisfied with the progress on site, he returned to the White House to escort the press pool in the motorcade. I remained at the site to complete preparations and direct any press arriving independently.

The National Archives are located north of the National Mall on Constitution Avenue. Among other government documents, the archives house the original documents of our nation's founding: the Declaration of Independence, Bill of Rights, and the Constitution. The main hall, the Rotunda for the Charters of Freedom, also displays the 1297 Magna Carta, the Louisiana Purchase Treaty, and the Emancipation Proclamation. This night the archives were alive with activity. I was surprised at the number of Secret Service agents, fifty or sixty of them, and how young and well-dressed they all were. There was a SWAT team, in olive drab complete with machine guns in fitted cases, that took position on the roof, and a swarm of bomb squad agents.

Security was particularly tight because so many high-level officials would be together in one spot. I was given a five-cent tin pin to fold over my lapel for identification. Steve had a permanent staff pin, brass and enamel, which I coveted. The Secret Service used a lapel-sized replica of their five-pointed star badges. I had a green tin "S," the symbol and color of the day for a temporary staff pin. It seemed to scream out "mere volunteer," but the Secret Service treated me professionally.

After the preparations were complete, the bomb squad "swept" the building—searched the entire area with electronic detectors and dogs trained to smell explosives. I watched the dogs circle the room while the handlers directed them to examine every feature. I asked one of the agents how they knew when a dog had smelled a bomb. "The dog will sit, and refuse to move," he said.

Shortly after that, I was on the receiving end of my first Secret Service hazing. As the dog handler casually trotted the dog past me, the dog promptly sat by my leg and refused to move. The agents, watching my startled reaction, all laughed.

"The president is coming tonight," the dog handler noted.

I nodded.

"You polished your shoes?"

I realized I had.

He clapped me on the shoulder with a smile, "The shoe polish has some of the same compounds the dogs are trained to recognize. Happens every time."

My breathing returned. The event was a whirlwind of bands, security agents, press, dignitaries, color guards, and the public. Steve Studdert and I choreographed our pool moves like practiced dance partners. Several times Steve nodded silent approval as I created one-at-a-time cutaway angles for the pool photographers. The White House staff in the VIP viewing area gave us a thumbs-up.

I was already on a high when I left the building after the departure of the motorcade. I was pulling my earpiece off as I crossed the street when I noticed a little boy looking up at me with an expression of awe. Perhaps I wasn't as young or well-dressed enough to be a Secret Service agent, but he obviously thought I was. I crouched down to match his level, "Would you like a Secret Service ID pin?" I asked.

I saw him look up at his dad, his eyes widening. Dad nodded. I pinned my tin pin on the front of his shirt. The little boy burst into tears of joy and pride.

His tears touched me as much as they did him. I had spent the night in close company of senior White House and congressional officials, much of the time only a few feet from President Ford, but it was the reaction of that little boy that really drove home how privileged I was to be part of this historic occasion.

\* \* \*

The next night was the closing event of the bicentennial, "Honor America Night" at the Kennedy Center, where Steve and I did it all again. We sat next to the presidential box for the performance where we rotated pool members to record Bob

Hope, Telly Savalas, Art Linkletter, Annette Funicello, O.J. Simpson, and George Kennedy from our balcony overlooking the stage. The press interspersed cutaway shots of President Ford reacting. The show was fun. Everyone seemed delighted. Steve and I left with a new friendship and warm satisfaction.

The two-hundredth birthday of America will always be a special memory.

The next couple of weeks included the Republican National Convention, so those of us back in Washington had some quiet time. I caught up on the projects at my *real* job.

When President Ford returned from his narrow victory over Ronald Reagan for the nomination, he was eager to get to work. Assigned with a variety of leads—David Wendell, Dorrance Smith, and Dave Frederickson—I advanced a flurry of in-town speeches. The most memorable event was a German Embassy Reception for chancellor Helmut Schmidt onboard the *Gorch Fock,* the German tall ship, in Baltimore Harbor. Dave Frederickson and I spent the whole day setting up the press center, pool pens, and platforms. We turned the restaurant boat, *Nobska,* into an office for Ron Nessen and a press filing center, with three dozen telephones, duplicating machines, typewriters (remember those?), and UPI and AP teletypes. Little by little we brought the historic Baltimore Inner Harbor to a standstill.

The German sailors did a special welcoming ceremony for their chancellor, a "Yard Arm" drill, where hundreds of cadets climbed the masts to salute from the high cross trees all the way to the sky. Quite a sight.

Just as President Ford was to arrive, we had a huge downpour. I was completely exposed on the pier, so I just had to grin and bear it as the motorcade approached with lights and sirens. I looked like a limp dishrag in my soaked three-piece suit. Somehow the Secret Service still looked crisp and well-dressed.

As the dignitaries mingled aboard the *Gorch Fock,* most of the press were confined to a pen near the gangway, so I kept them apprised of the president's movements by listening to the Secret Service updates on "Passkey," Gerald Ford's Secret Service code name.

President Ford was a naturally kind and considerate man. Before departing, he came over to speak to the dripping press corps. He noticed me in my tin pin and ruined suit and said, "Get up on that ship and enjoy some champagne."

The rest of the evening was a short but enjoyable stint at an embassy party, with the tall ships decked in lights as a backdrop. No one commented on my dripping clothes.

As August ended, the 1976 presidential campaign loomed.

* * *

I would run into Steve Studdert on and off for the next twenty years, as he became the first director of advance for President Reagan, advised the 1984 Reagan campaign, and managed George H. W. Bush's 1989 inauguration. It was always a pleasure to see him.

Dorrance Smith later began a long-running career as producer of "This Week with David Brinkley."

# Learning the Ropes

## Gerald Ford Campaign

### 1976

By now, the initial novelty had worn off. I still felt awe while entering the power centers of Washington, still felt a satisfaction that I was contributing to a patriotic mission, but the demands were causing a strain on my work relationships and even my family life. For months, every evening, weekend, and holiday had been co-opted. As the real campaign approached, I was beginning to ask myself if I wanted to continue such a sacrifice.

Then I received a letter on impressive White House stationery inviting me to an advance seminar over the Labor Day weekend, killing another holiday. Doug Blaser added a handwritten note saying he had arranged enough money to add me to the staff full time for the two months of the campaign. I took a breath. Full-time staff.

This called for a family summit. My wife, Pat, would have the only vote that counted.

When I showed her the letter, Pat was immediately supportive: "You should be honored that they selected you instead of one of the dozens of volunteers they must have had over the months of the primaries and convention."

I *was* honored, but I was also putting my employment at GEICO on the line. Even if I combined all of my vacation time, I could only do a month. Would GEICO grant me a leave? What would they think about my commitment to my job? Would my staff and responsibilities tolerate a two-month absence? Was I ready to leave GEICO? Everything was reexamined in light of this new opportunity. Pat and I concluded it was a bridge too far.

Finally I reluctantly called Doug Blaser to say I could not do two months, so I would have to pass on the paid position. He was abrupt: "I'll have to go to the next on my list to get the job done." He was noticeably irked that I hadn't jumped at the offer.

"Sorry, Doug," I said, feeling lame. "I'd still like to do what I can."

After a pause he said, "Come to the damn seminar."

The advance seminar restored my commitment in every way. Top brass from the White House, including the president, participated in our orientation. I was ashamed that I had been reluctant to give up Labor Day.

At first I was ill at ease. The fifteen recruits seemed to be over-represented with Mormons, lawyers, and Southerners. Most were imposing and high-powered, an intimidating group, but I wagered that I had done more presidential events, albeit small ones, than any of the others, and most of them were new to Washington. They began to gravitate to me for information. We bonded easily over lunch in the White House mess.

The first day was a series of lectures from old hands in a White House conference room. Terry O'Donnell spoke about President Ford as a man (patient, gregarious, loves crowds and people, hates to ever disappoint anyone by not showing, likes the press and understands their problems and viewpoints). Dick Kaiser, the head of the Presidential Protection detail of the Secret Service, spoke about the security viewpoint (agents had usually spent several years as "street cops," but were college-educated. We might expect some "tests of ego" with them, but they have very high determination in a very difficult job). David Gergen, head of White House Communications, gave us a detailed briefing on campaign strategy.

We watched film from events showing advance men in action, and critiqued some notable disasters. Then we all boarded a bus for the Washington Navy Yard. It soon became apparent we were being directed to the presidential yacht, *Sequoia*. We passed through a gauntlet of saluting Navy men for a cruise and dinner aboard the presidential yacht. What a wonderful surprise.

We cruised down the Potomac while a guide gave us some history about the boat and the impressive events that had occurred onboard: FDR and Eisenhower had planned D-Day, Truman had hosted poker parties, Nixon decided to resign his presidency, and President Kennedy's last birthday party had been held on the *Sequoia*. We pinched ourselves as we dined among the ghosts of a half-dozen administrations dating from Herbert Hoover. We left impressed with the reverence the Navy bestowed on this hallowed vessel, a unique treasure of American history.

The next day, the pleasant surprises kept coming. After a long, excellent session by Dorrance Smith about the typical problems that come up and how to prepare for them (always have the house electrician on hand, have keys for every door you are likely to encounter, don't surprise the Secret Service, *always* have a plan B), Terry O'Donnell took us on an extended tour of the White House. We sat in the Cabinet Room, strolled the Oval Office and the president's private study, stood at the press podium in the media center, and visited Ron Nessen's office and the Rose Garden.

As we reentered the White House, we were startled to be met by President Ford in the Diplomatic Reception Room. After a brief pep talk, he chatted with each of us and posed for individual pictures. We each received a signed copy of Ford's Bicentennial Fourth of July speeches and a set of presidential cufflinks.

Doug Blaser finished with a little heart-felt discourse about how "money could not buy the kind of experiences we would have over the next few months." He actually got choked up talking about it, which I found charming.

Politicians really know how to seal the deal.

As I left, I was handed an airplane ticket for the next morning . . . my first campaign trip.

\* \* \*

Jimmy Carter sold the *Sequoia* in 1977 as a cost-cutting measure.

# HERO FOR A DAY

I had reached agreement with my company to spend a week on the campaign, followed by a week in the office; that way my accrued vacation time would stretch for nearly the full two months of the campaign. I flew into New York on Labor Day to begin preparations for Senator Robert Dole's first appearance as the vice presidential candidate.

It was somewhat of a letdown to be assigned to the veep candidate, but it was impressed on me that Dole had no staff, so it would take our "best men" to jump-start his appearances from scratch. I was promised trips with the president later in the campaign. David Wendell, one of our best full-timers, was put in charge of the Dole press advance effort back in headquarters.

Little did I know what shambles headquarters was in: campaign staffers thought they were in charge but a new influx of seasoned White House hands and honchos from Dole's senate staff challenged most decisions. Lining up volunteers for the road was chaotic, with poor Barbara McCaffery, the ramrod of the road trips, using guile, seduction, and shameless persuasion to assemble a combination of aides from the primary campaign and ex-Reagan advancemen.

More of a concern to me was that there would be no WHCA support for the vice presidential candidate, so no provided podium, radios, sound system, or mult box. Even Secret Service support was at a much lower level than for the president—all understandable, but it meant everything would be harder.

Our event was a speech before the Zionist Organization of America in the Grand Ballroom of the Waldorf Astoria. My primary challenges would be lighting, press platform, media advisories, and press credentials. The Zionist Organization provided several attractive volunteers to handle our phones, but they spent most of their time on their own association work—another lesson learned.

I was supposed to be working with Bob Tuttle, the staff advance (lead), but our ten o'clock meeting time passed with no word. So I set about releasing the time and requirements for press credentials, and negotiated a deal with one of the New York television stations to supply the lighting for eight hundred and fifty dollars. I gave the hotel carpenters my requirements for the press platform, and construction began immediately. By three o'clock, still no Tuttle, which meant no schedule, no budget, no direction, and I was already spending his money.

Finally Tuttle called to say he had been delayed by a train derailment (the dog ate my homework). He asked me to come to his room. From his casual arrival, I was expecting a turkey, but Tuttle was far from it. He was tanned, distinguished, mid-forties with an unmistakable air of authority. In between a constant stream of phone calls, he introduced me to Rob St. Clair, his site advanceman, who was shorter, balding, not so self-assured, but friendly. We chatted while waiting for Bob to get free. I learned that Tuttle and St. Clair had been with Reagan "from the snows of New Hampshire" and came to Dole's staff after the convention. I did not mention that my heart had been with Reagan's challenge even though my duty had been to Gerald Ford. Both of our commitments had brought us to a presidential campaign.

Tuttle turned from the phone and said, "So, you're from the White House Press Office." He was smooth and pleasant, but he was leading into a pre-emptive strike. He went on to say, "I haven't had much luck working with White House advancemen, because they fail to recognize there can only be one boss."

I saw the humiliated look on Rob's face, but I just chuckled, "Good to meet you too." We all smiled. I guess he was satisfied he had made his point. He passed out the draft schedule and we all got to work as a massive room-service cart rolled into the room. I stopped feeling guilty about my eight hundred and fifty dollar lighting bill.

The next day started with a standard ritual: a walk-through with the Secret Service. We covered the entire route the candidate would follow, from the Marine Air Terminal at La Guardia to the Waldorf, then the back corridors of the hotel to the suite, the ballroom, the holding rooms, and the press center. Tuttle and the Secret Service both seemed pleased that I had started the press accreditation process so they would not have to worry about it. Lead agent Bill MacClain provided me with Jim Ryan, a very good agent, to run background checks on the applicants for credentials. When we got to the ballroom, the press platform was already nearly completed. Tuttle and St. Clair exchanged surprised glances. I was gaining points.

Now the search for a mult box took on the aura of a quest for the Holy Grail. A mult box eliminates the sea of haphazardly attached microphones on the podium. It is a rare, or at least not stock, piece of audio gear that allows multiple connections from a single mike. Every video or radio crew can connect at the press platform without the need to run their own cable and mike to the podium. Neat, easy, fast. WHCA always brought the mult box, but we had no WHCA. Rob St. Clair had unsuccessfully called every radio and television outlet in New York City. No mult boxes. Many had never even heard of a mult box. Rob and Bob turned the quest over to me like an initiation challenge (to dream the impossible dream).

Fortunately, I had an ace up my sleeve. Corporations with frequent press briefings sometimes had mult boxes, and back in my GEICO office, I had a list of New York City corporations who were members of the Industrial Television Association. My secretary read it to me. I started with the most likely suspects, and, by the fifth call, had the sign-off from Exxon to borrow their mult box.

When I carried it into the staff office just before dinner, I experienced a welcome somewhat like Caesar's triumphant return to Rome. Now I knew I had breached the inner circle with Rob and Bob. Arm in arm, we all went off to dinner for an evening of war stories and bonding.

D-Day Our First Dole Campaign Stop
New York City
September 10, 1976


We had a bullpen set up at the Marine Air Terminal where a few local press waited. An old Cadillac arrived, festooned with four-inch white walls, hearse-like bunting across the hood, and embassy-style American flags on the front fenders. The rumpled driver declared he was sent to pick up Senator Dole. "I always drive the Republican candidates when they come to New York." Suppressing our horror, we directed him to the end of the motorcade. Rob explained that we had an armored limo for the senator from the Secret Service, but if the driver took off the bunting and flags, he could transport the "senior staff." The driver could have starred in his own comedy routine as, belching clouds of smoke, he repeatedly drove up on the curb or otherwise failed to properly position the car. The plane landed before we had a chance to reconsider the whole idea.

Comedy turned to chaos in short order. A stream of reporters poured out of the back of the senator's plane on a dead run for the front door, where the senator, looking tired and pinched, went directly to his limo. The schedule called for him to answer questions briefly at the press pen. He didn't. The reporters made a U-turn and ran for the press bus, lovingly stocked with sandwiches and beer by their talented advance team. I frantically gathered the pool. We ran for our cars and were off.

What a sideshow. Rush-hour traffic in New York City; a single police car at the head of the line; no control at the intersections (as was commonly in place for the president). Every man for himself.

New York drivers are decidedly unimpressed by a police-led motorcade. As soon as the police car passed, they tried to cut in to speed up their commute. Soon our nine-car motorcade had become a twenty-car motorcade. Only the steaming old Cadillac kept the commuters at bay by depositing a smoke screen behind us.

What followed was a series of near misses as we lurched and charged across town to Manhattan from LaGuardia, all of us hanging on for dear life. When we got to Manhattan, we grimly tailgated the car in front to make it through stoplights as side street traffic aggressively charged at us if the light changed. I'm not sure how we made it, but a measure of our slow pace is that the press bus beat us to the hotel.

At last, safety. Things should have calmed down, but they didn't. The reporters headed for the press center, but the sandwiches had been left on the bus. (I sent a volunteer for them.) The press wanted a television set so they could watch the evening news. (I should have thought of it. The hotel provided one.) Fifteen people showed up who wanted press credentials, twenty-four hours after the deadline. (Secret Service agent Jim Ryan dealt with them.) From the press platform, the senator's seat on the ballroom stage was hidden behind the dais. (I moved it to the other side.) Otherwise, everything was great.

The press munched sandwiches and watched television. Senator Dole met with local officials in his suite, then on to the ballroom for the main event.

The lighting, mult box, and position of the press platform were all perfect. David Wendell kept flashing me pleased nods. The senator's speech was well received, but seemed stiff and canned to me. It dragged in the middle, and was totally devoid of sound bites.

Dole remained for some time after the speech to sign autographs, while the press went up to file; then it was the same crazy motorcade back to the airport. This time, we got separated at a red light. It was a semi race from that point with no rhyme or order. In the midst of the confusion, we came upon the "staff" limo-of-the-four-inch-whitewalls. It was steaming from all sides, broken down completely at the tollbooth. Amid much laughter and joking, we picked up the stragglers, leaving the poor rumpled driver to fend for himself.

We arrived at the plane, where by some miracle, everyone had made it. I was flying back to Washington on the senator's plane along with Bob Tuttle and David Wendell. Everyone was feeling happy. The job was done. It had been a fair success.

Tuttle said he was going to request me for all of his trips. David Wendell said he was calling GEICO from the plane to get me fired so I could stay on the campaign. Wendell took me forward to shake hands with Senator Dole and to meet his wife. "Terry was the press advance for this trip," David said by way of introduction.

"Good speech," I mumbled insincerely.

"It was too long," Dole replied gruffly, "just about five minute too long."

"More like twenty minutes too long," I said.

No, actually I didn't say anything. I just stood there awkwardly while Dole beckoned for his speechwriter. Dole's press aide, Janet Anderson, shook my hand. Elizabeth Dole offered me a kindly smile, while the speechwriter hurried over to take his medicine. Eventually I found the opportunity to slip away.

This is called accessing the corridors of power.

Basking in self-satisfaction and accolades, I went home with no hint of the disaster the next trip would bring.

# September Chaos

It was heaven to have a weekend at home. My son Bryan and I spent Saturday in the garage, carving, sanding, and painting a block of wood for the Cub Scouts' Pinewood Derby. By late evening, we had produced a sleek wooden race car—just in time. The big event was Wednesday night. On Sunday, Bryan surprised me by painting the number 27 on the car, the number from one of my winning race cars memorialized in his photo album marked "Dad."

I managed to log one entire day at GEICO (my job, remember), when Barbara McCaffrey called me. Her words were rushed; her voice was urgent. From what I was able to gather, the campaign headquarters had been a shambles for the previous week. The Ford White House people got fed up about the lack of ability in the headquarters and staged a walk out. After a day of panic and recriminations, they were ordered back to work, but at the expense of the Reagan group, now incensed at the liberties given the Ford people, so *they* walked out, maybe for good. Dole's Senate staff had flooded the headquarters with helpful directives to have "warm tea with honey in every holding room," and "butterbrickle ice cream in every hotel suite." They also reminded us that advancemen should be invisible. The senator had no "handlers." They added with a sniff, "*Mere advancemen* did not raise crowds, Senator Dole *drew* crowds."

All of this was background to the new crisis. "New Jersey," Barbara wailed. "You have no choice. You *have* to go to New Jersey right away."

I reminded her that I was supposed to be at GEICO for the week. That was my deal. One week on, one week off.

"No one else can do it. Leave your job and your family and go at once. The New Jersey trip is a disaster. You won't believe what terrible advancemen are up there."

"Who?" I asked in all innocence.

"Tuttle and St. Clair!"

"Oh my God," I said reflexively, while I wondered how two such good advancemen could have earned this bad rap back at headquarters. "What's the problem?"

"I don't know for sure, but Tom Andrews is up there—you know him from the seminar—and he is having such a bad time with Tuttle and St. Clair that he called Doug Blaser at three in the morning to complain they are freezing him out. Blaser treated headquarters to a scorched-earth visit this morning. Our ears are still ringing. So, go to New Jersey for Doug."

I reluctantly agreed. In New Jersey, Tom Andrews and Gregg Stevens met me in the lobby of the Ramada Inn. Tom obviously wanted to intercept me at once. While there were a few obvious duds at the seminar, I had pegged Tom as smart and able. He was about forty-two, nice looking, and seemingly intelligent, but transparently arrogant. Now he was red-faced and overflowing with testosterone.

Gregg Stevens was a local, the press secretary for the New Jersey Republican Committee. Stocky, well-dressed, and calm. Compared to Tom's about-to-erupt volcano, Gregg made a good first impression. They led me to the staff office for a debriefing.

Tom launched into a litany of complaints about the slights he had endured in an overblown and overly officious manner. He told me that Tuttle had been completely uncooperative, and had been out of contact for the entire day. But he didn't have time to talk about it, he had "very important things to do" at the site. He left with a purposeful stride.

As calm settled on the room, Gregg and I looked at each other with relief. "Well, that clears things up," I said. We both laughed. I asked Gregg for his assessment. He bemoaned being the man in the middle—Tuttle and Andrews each had told him not to listen to the other side—but Tom Andrews was the problem as he saw it, popping off about everything under the sun and unwilling to listen to advice. I thanked him for his candor, but I had no idea how to improve the situation.

We turned to press issues. Gregg had things well in hand, a good state organization, an already staffed press office, credentials underway, and he had contacted most of the key media himself. The event had three stops: a Menlo Park Shopping Mall walk-through, a luncheon speech at the hotel before the Jaycees (the US Junior Chamber, an active social and civic organization for young businessmen), and a speech at the New Jersey State Fair in Trenton. Gregg had a good start on all three. We all gathered for dinner at ten, a relatively common practice for advance teams. Tuttle and St. Clair greeted me warmly, which made Tom Andrews visibly squirm. Bob

Tuttle and Rob St. Clair began reviewing the outline of the events, while Tom frequently interrupted with suggestions for "improving Dole's image" or "spicing up his speeches." These might be relevant topics for the national campaign staff, but did little to hasten our advance preparations. Each time Bob and Rob exchanged glances with me as if to say, "See?"

When asked about the press arrangements, Tom said, "We need a priest to greet Dole at the airport, a neutral party to give him credibility." Eyes glazed over. As Cool Hand Luke would have observed, "What we got here is a failure to communicate." When I got back to my room, Tom had already been on the phone to headquarters complaining. Steve Studdert called me to say, "Don't get rolled by Tuttle." Being rolled, as in "steamrolled," is an anathema to advancemen—railroaded into a decision not in the best interest of the trip. I sighed, but refused to enter the contest of egos.

"Steve," I said, "we are all on the same side." I am not sure I believed it as I said it.

The next call was from Pat. It was nice to hear a friendly voice after Studdert's strident warnings, but I caught an edge in Pat's voice too. "Pinewood Derby," she said.

"Oh no," I groaned, "I forgot. You'll take him?"

"Of course."

"Tell him I'm sorry."

"He knows."

"I'm sorry, Pat."

"I know too."

The next morning, Rob St. Clair and I went to the Trenton fairgrounds. The fairgrounds are also the site of the Indy car races, with an oval track surrounded by huge grandstands, so I was excited to meet the owner, George Hamid. He was garrulous and decisive. He mustered his forces like a general. He greeted each of my requests by picking up the phone and directing the recipient to "take charge of this detail."

Bill Gross, the commander of the New Jersey VFW, arrived in Hamid's office like one of Hamid's minions. I learned that Tuttle and St. Clair had arranged for Dole to be the grand marshal of the annual VFW parade, a motorcade of antique cars circling the speedway with the veterans wildly cheering from the grandstands. As Gross appeared increasingly overwhelmed by the needs to sweep the grandstands for security and inspect each of the cars, I directed him to the Secret Service to iron it out. Rob was working with him on signs and flags for the crowd as I left.

I walked the site of the main speech, just at the entrance to the speedway, where the platform faced away from the back of the grandstands into the main arcade of the fairgrounds. Bill Sharp was Hamid's construction chief. We agreed on all the requirements: the press platform, the speaker's platform, the power, the sound system, and he arranged for a decorator to erect signs, banners, and flags everywhere. He was a godsend. A productive morning.

Then the lions started roaring. Circus lions. They were housed in cages under the grandstands for a lion-taming show, and, every once in awhile, they would initiate feline disputes—strikingly similar to our advance team. The shrieking was louder than any speech would be, and probably more interesting. Bill Sharp wasn't sure they could be relocated. I called Barbara McCaffrey to tell her the site was questionable until I confirmed the lions could be moved. She took it in stride.

When I got back to New Brunswick, a new crisis had emerged. Tom Andrews had made the hotel manager so angry he had ordered his crew to tear down the press platform in the Jaycees' luncheon room. Tuttle had tried to talk to the manager, Mr. Metzger, but the man was intransigent. "You go talk to Metzger," Tuttle told me. "You are a new face, plus you're such a smoothie. I know you can charm this guy." Andrews hovered in the background with a smirk that said, "Good luck, hot shot."

I went to Metzger's office feeling like the sacrificial lamb. He sat behind his desk with a huge cigar. He looked up with no obvious desire to kill.

"Excuse me, Mr. Metzger, could I talk to you for a moment?"

"Sure, have a seat." He had a pronounced wise-guy accent, and his eyes were out of alignment so that he seemed to be looking in two directions at once. I sat down and tried to decide which eye to look into.

"I've just arrived to help with the Dole appearance. I've been told there's a bit of a problem with one of our guys."

"You can say that again. I don't even want to see that little twerp around here anymore."

"Who do you mean?"

"This Andrews guy. Who needs it."

Just to be safe, I shifted slightly to focus on his other eye. "Maybe you could tell me what the problem is. I'll get Andrews out of your hair."

Metzger sat forward in his chair. I hoped there wasn't a gun in his desk drawer. "Listen, I've been dealing with the Jaycees on this conference for months. We got everything all straight. Then fancy-pants Dole is going to come speak. Your guys come charging in here, no notice, no conversation, just change this, change that. When I try to talk to your man, he says, 'This is the way it's going to be.' And he thinks I'm going to listen to that? He never once came in to say, 'Hello, maybe you could help me.' No, right away he's giving orders like he owns the place, owns me. To hell with him."

"Okay, Mr. Metzger. I agree. That's not acceptable. I'm just going to send Andrews home."

Metzger's eyebrows shot up. His various eyes brightened. He sat back in his chair again, tension escaping.

"Now," I continued, "maybe if you have a moment, you could show me the problem with the room."

He bounced up, friendly and almost contrite. He led me to the ballroom and showed me how the press platform and the center aisle Tom had demanded displaced four or five tables of paying customers.

"I see the problem," I nodded. *I feel your pain.*

He told his men to stop dismantling the press platform. "Hey guys, hold on a minute." He turned to me, conciliatory. "Maybe we could just move the platform against the wall," he suggested.

The angle and the throw would be off. But that was my problem. I tried to think of *his* problem. "I'm trying to see it from your standpoint, Mr. Metzger. We'd need much more lighting with the platform that far away. I personally think it would be more disturbing to your guests—maybe even a safety hazard—to have a dozen more lights on stands scattered among the crowd." I looked up toward the ceiling and swayed like I was watching the teetering lights. "It would be hotter in here, too. I'd really like to avoid that, if we can."

I could see the vision of all those hot lights was weighing heavily on him. He looked up, eyes going in four directions. "Well, maybe I could open this alcove and put some tables in there . . ."

"Say, that would be great," I said. He was starting to solve his own problem. I decided to extend the olive branch that Tuttle had suggested. "What if we brought the senator in behind the speaker's platform instead of up this center aisle? Without the aisle, you might get all your tables in the main room."

"That's good! That's a great idea." He snapped his fingers. "Then everything's okay." He wiped his brow like a great weight had been lifted.

We shook hands. He seemed very happy. I was amazed it had been so easy.

"Oh," he turned to me, "don't fire the kid. I've had a bad couple of weeks. Just a little on edge. But, if there are any more questions for the hotel, I'd appreciate if you would handle them."

I nodded. I had to work hard to subdue my euphoria as I walked into the dining room. The team was watching the door as if I would return with my clothes shredded. Tom's jaw dropped as he heard the problems had been resolved, then his expression turned to a sulk. I realized he was concerned I would belittle his efforts when talking to Washington—he obviously didn't comprehend that I didn't spend all my time on the phone to headquarters. "It was surely just a new face that made a difference with Metzger. You guys had already softened him up," I said by way of a peace offering.

We made our way back to our rooms through a raucous crowd. The evening before the visit, and the hotel was crammed with party-mad, rip-roaring, flap-jawed Jaycees. A long, noisy night.

* * *

D Day, and the plans started to implode. Dole's plane was late, so everything got set back an hour. Then at the mall walk-through, some bystander made some threatening remark, and the Secret Service "wrestled him to the ground." The press stopped to cover the melee, missing the press bus to New Brunswick. Most of them arrived too late to hear Dole's speech.

Then the meltdown.

The fairgrounds arrival was sloppy. Rob had arrived late and was gathering the band while the motorcade pulled in without him noticing. I got the press to the platform and the senator to Hamid's office, where we regrouped over hot tea and honey. Fortunately the crowd was still a reasonable size, even with an hour extra wait. The site looked good and the speech was better than the one in New York. No lions roared (I had moved them).

But the VFW parade was a total disaster. Rob got rolled by the Secret Service. They decided they could not admit veterans to the stadium until after Dole spoke at the arcade because it would allow hard-to-secure people to enter a structure behind the speaking platform.

Dole lingered briefly after the speech to shake hands, then went to the antique car motorcade to sit with Commander Gross in the back of an open convertible. I had an antique pick-up truck to serve as the camera car behind Dole. The marching band formed up at the head of the parade, and we all made our two-mile-per-hour entrance into the Indy car oval.

Years later, my friend Jim Hooley played me the audio tape of a radio reporter riding in the camera car. "And we are entering the Trenton Speedway for the VFW tribute to Senator Dole. The band is playing, the grandstands are massive and . . . oh my God, there is no one here . . . the stands are completely empty . . ."

Actually, there were little knots of veterans, with more trickling slowly through the Secret Service checkpoint, but in the vast grandstands they were lost. Senator Dole, live on camera, was trapped in his slowly moving motorcade, smiling and waving to a sea of empty grandstands all the way around the Trenton mile.

By the time he was back in the limo, Dole was seething.

It was a long trip home.

As word of our fiasco spread through the advance community, the standard joke became, "Who advanced that trip?" The punch line: "Obviously no one."

# MAKING SAUSAGE

David Wendell called me before 8 a.m. at GEICO the next morning. I felt surely the ax was falling, but instead he said, "We need an expert here in the headquarters to answer questions these inexperienced advancemen are asking from the road. You are the first person I thought of."

Really? *The campaign's expert on lighting and staging after two stops? Wow.* "I'll be happy to help," I said with pleasure. "You can have anyone with questions call me here at work," I said.

"Sorry, that won't do it. We need someone right in the headquarters . . ." I heard Barbara McCaffrey in the background saying, "Tell him I need to see him down here today." Ah, this must be my invitation to the gallows. I agreed to come during lunchtime.

I met Rob St. Clair on the street outside headquarters with another advanceman, Dave Harris. They said hello but looked glum, fellow death-row inmates perhaps.

Campaign headquarters was a haphazard jumble of desks and cubicles, each over-populated by eager young workers. I first found Steven Studdert then nearby, David Wendell and Barbara McCaffrey, all on the phone.

I sat down to wait for Barbara. David was speaking earnestly into the phone, "I have to go on the road. I need someone we can trust to coordinate all the phones here in the headquarters. You are the first person I thought of . . ."

In the next cubicle, Barbara was recruiting advancemen for an upcoming Dole trip. "No one else can do it," she pleaded.

I chuckled to myself. Had I been the same easy mark for such obvious plays to my ego? Of course I had. I had been a prime sucker. I felt naïve, manipulated, and, well, human, but the scales had dropped from my eyes.

A voice from another cubicle groaned, "Scanlon says he will never work another stop with Harvey . . . if we ever get a team that can work together, it will be a miracle." I wanted to say, "Hey, we have a team that works together perfectly," but I stifled myself. Barbara divorced herself from her phone and beckoned me. She talked to me in a conspiratorial whisper. "Dole was livid after New Jersey. He told us to fire *everyone* connected to the trip."

My shoulders sagged.

She put her hand on my arm. "Three things saved you. First, you went up there for Doug Blaser. Second, you called to question the site."

"Yeah, well, that was because of the lions, remember?"

"No, I don't remember, and you don't either." She fixed me with a *wise up* look. "You questioned the site, and third, you were the *press* advance, not the site or lead, so no termination. We're sending you out again tomorrow."

"I'm happy to be spared, but I can't go out tomorrow. This is the week for my company. I have to stick to my promise."

She looked stricken by my ingratitude, but nodded.

\* \* \*

After the Democratic Convention where Jimmy Carter was nominated, President Ford trailed by more than thirty points in the polls. Carter presented himself as a "Washington outsider." The public, weary of Watergate and Ford's pardon of Nixon, was ready to turn the page. The press traveling with us considered the campaign a lost cause. The rumors of the campaign disarray confirmed their attitudes.

The *Washington Star* reported on September 21 under the headline "Dole's Staff Undergoes A Shakeup":

> Sen. Bob Dole's vice-presidential campaign staff has undergone a shakeup because of catch-as-catch-can scheduling and poor advancework . . . (the campaign) declined to say how many staff members were fired or to identify them, but said it was more than two persons . . . the final event that "brought it all to a head" was a motorcade at a New Jersey fair last week.

I felt embarrassed reading it. *The Washington Post* reported the next day:

> The (campaign) disorganization reached comic proportions. In Boston Thursday, the press bus—a foul-smelling antiquated vehicle—was too high to fit through several underpasses on the way to the event.
>
> It had to back out of a two-lane highway the wrong way, police sirens screeching . . . the press missed Dole's speech.

At least this second disaster wasn't one of our events, but I felt a disappointing certainty that Bob Tuttle and Rob St. Clair were part of the "more than two people" who were fired. Maybe me too for all I knew. That night was the first of two presidential debates. I thought both candidates were uninspiring, but the general consensus was that Ford won the debate, which began a slow rise in the polls for our campaign.

I was soon to find out I was still part of it.

# CRUNCH TIME

## THIRTY-FIVE CITIES IN TEN DAYS

### OCTOBER 1976

With a little more than a month to go, the campaign went into hyper-drive. Advances were shortened to two or three days. I was scheduled directly to my next city before the balloons had been cleared from the current campaign site. All pretense of a week in the office was abandoned. GEICO generously accommodated me.

I was teamed up with a new lead, Pam Laudenslager. Partly as a warning to me, it was explained that Laudenslager had been demoted from the president's team to Dole's as a result of an injudicious interview she gave, which resulted in the headline, "She tells the president what to do." I almost laughed when I heard that. Interviews with the press are always a minefield. Comments taken out of context have created a thousand headlines. It was easy to imagine how innocent remarks about schedules and diagrams could lead to a reporter's hyperbole. Poor Pam. I struggled to appear sufficiently chastened by the cautionary tale.

Half expecting to find Laudenslager sullen and resentful, I joined her in the staff office in Decatur, America's Heartland. On the contrary, she was cheerful and confidently in charge. Nothing about being a lead intimidated her. Pam was tall and loose-limbed, with a toothy smile and friendly manner. I immediately felt comfortable. Site advance was a sexy bleached blonde, Sandy Blair, who spoke in a deep Texas drawl and chewed gum incessantly. We fell into our roles with an easy rhythm.

By now, I had a regular bag of tricks to solve some of my usual problems. I carried my own small lighting kit. The campaign had finally produced a mult box. For volunteers, I often called the local college to recruit television students, which I had been merely a decade before. I knew that students, regardless of political affiliation, would relish the chance to participate in a presidential or even vice-presidential campaign stop, to witness the press operation up close and to collect one more star for their resumés. When I called the head of a college television department to invite some students to be part of a White House press advance, the response was usually enthusiastic.

I should admit here that I was incredibly naïve about the broader political context of a campaign. I thought of myself as helping the president, the White House, or even in moments of immodesty, the nation. I had no real political agenda. I had no input to strategy or policy matters. I admired President Ford, but I had morphed from assisting with the bicentennial and official presidential appearances to campaign events with no more ambition than to do my duty.

This time my phone call seeking volunteers had been directed to Dr. Scott at the local college. He cheerfully agreed to send several promising students. My first volunteer was Phil

Chapel, a young black man with a huge Afro, who was dressed like a Hell's Angel. Sandy Blair nearly swallowed her gum. A short interview revealed Phil was smart, energetic, and perfectly willing to dress more appropriately on the day of the event. He turned out to be one of my mainstays for the trip, full of local knowledge and contacts.

I later discovered that Dr. Scott was a Democrat precinct captain. Perhaps he hoped my reaction to Phil would create an awkward incident. Maybe I just have an overactive imagination. I would find out that Dr. Scott had other traps in store.

Over dinner at the Blue Mill, or as Sandy called it, "the Bloo Meal," the girls and I lamented the lack of cohesion on the Dole team. Pam described how President Ford always sought her out after a trip to say thanks, but Dole never said one word to her. Sandy had heard Dole never wanted to even *see* an advanceman. "If he ever laid eyes on you, you are fired," was the way she put it. She planned to spend the event hiding behind bushes and columns.

"And he hates to hear the words, 'the White House,'" Pam added. "He once fired an aide on the spot because he introduced himself as 'from the White House.'"

My stomach turned over. Dr. Scott, the head of the Television Department (and as of yet unknown-to-me Democrat precinct captain), invited me to address his media students. He also had an afternoon television talk show where he wanted to interview me. I should have heeded the Laudenslager headline debacle, but my ego took over. I enjoyed talking to students. I agreed to both.

The classroom visit was pure pleasure. The students were bright, interested, and asked insightful questions. I gained a new volunteer, Brian Noe, the picture of a perfect recruit: intelligent and responsible, nicely dressed, eager and enthusiastic. Brian Noe and Phil Chapel were two of the best volunteers I had in 1976.

Then Dr. Scott led me to his television studio with a miniature version of Johnny Carson's set. Casual happy-talk ensued while we were miked, then his television persona emerged when the lights went up. "I am talking today with Terry Baxter, who is in town to advance Senator Dole's visit to Decatur." He turned to me with a practiced smile and said, "We first spoke about a week ago when you called about some volunteers."

"Yes," I agreed.

His face took on an artificial delirium. "And I was excited to think I was getting a call directly from the White House, right?"

The strange question set off alarm bells. The words "White House," which I knew I was guilty of dropping for their obvious value, could also grease the slides of Senator Dole's guillotine. "Well, sorry to disappoint you," I replied, "but I was calling from the campaign headquarters."

"But you mentioned the White House Press Advance Office, didn't you?"

"Yes. Of course, we coordinate our press accommodations with the Press Advance Office."

"So, do you work for the White House, or the campaign?"

Oh, I got it. He was hoping to insinuate that I was a government employee improperly doing political work.

"Actually, I am a volunteer just like the students you recommended for this visit. My real job is for GEICO, which has granted me leave. Before the campaign, I did some work for the White House Press Advance Office, but that was also volunteer. The bicentennial of the United States was a terrific experience."

The edge came out of his voice. I could tell he was frustrated, but he abandoned his "gotcha" inquiries. The rest of the interview was a pleasant living-room conversation. In spite of my momentary flop sweat, we parted as friends.

The Decatur event was a fine success. The crowd was respectable, the sites flowed well, and the press appreciated some photo ops we concocted. I saw a half-dozen students from my class visit, which pleased me. Of course there was a gaffe: the band played "Happy Days Are Here Again," Carter's campaign song. Across the room, Pam met my eyes with alarm, but the faux pas passed without comment. Sandy was safely hidden behind a nearby bush.

With barely a chance to say goodbye, Pam, Sandy, and I scattered like leaves before an autumn breeze as we each went on to new assignments in different cities. The comfort of a job well done went with us.

On the campaign plane, Janet Anderson, Mrs. Dole's chief of staff, noticed I still had a tin pin. "You've been on the campaign for weeks, you should have a permanent pin," she declared. She stomped off to the administrative czar and returned with a bronze-enameled staff pin. "Don't lose it. They are in short supply," she admonished me. "You just got the last one."

I have the pin in my treasure-box thirty-five years later. Janet probably had no idea how much I appreciated her thoughtfulness.

\* \* \*

When I stopped back at my office at GEICO for a quick cameo visit, the door was labeled "STORAGE" and the office filled with boxes. A little workplace humor.

The campaign ground on relentlessly. On October 6, President Ford committed a major blunder at the second presidential debate when he suggested that Eastern Europe was not under the domination of the Soviet Union. Press coverage for more than a week fixated on the debate, and Gerald Ford's surge in the polls plateaued. The campaign machinery had settled into a smooth operation, but the press traveling with us remained universally cynical and content to file paint-by-number reports about a losing effort.

Over the next five days, I went to Maine, New Hampshire, Connecticut, and Vermont. My new lead was Dann Stringer, a charming Cary Grant clone. Women swooned over him, men wanted to be him. He had an easy manner and a wry sense of humor. We immediately had fun together. We professionally turned out the expected stops—fundraisers, fairground visits, media events, rubber chicken dinners, and rallies.

As soon as I arrived in Portland, I began to hear that "Kotter is coming." I thought this meant the TV personality from *Welcome Back Kotter*, but it dawned on me eventually that they were saying "Carter," as in Jimmy Carter, who did indeed tour

Portland only a few days ahead of our Dole event. Dann and I went to see his airport arrival.

Carter paused at the door of his chartered airplane holding a suit bag over his shoulder. "Look," a woman behind us gushed, "he carries his own luggage."

Dann and I looked at each other in disbelief. Did people really believe such transparent sophistry? Didn't they notice the scores of bags being unloaded from the back of the plane? Carter looked good in person, but there was only a small crowd, and his speech sounded canned and mechanical. His movements were robotic and he smiled at inappropriate places. How could we be losing to this guy? When we went out that night, the bars were filled with Carter advancemen. After some prodding and flattery, one young staffer showed us his campaign manual where it demonstrated how to manipulate the television lighting to create a "radiant circle over Carter's head." We nodded sagely and winked. *Our secret.*

At our next stop, another young aide was in a circle of admirers, self-importantly sporting his tin pin and basking in celebrity. I sidled up to him and asked him, "Is that a Secret Service pin?" He beamed and nodded proudly.

"Are you a Secret Service agent?" I pressed, leaving an opening for him to escalate the puffery.

"No," he said, "I'm Kotter's chief campaign strategist in Maine."

"Wow," Dann and I said in unison. "Tell us how you are going to defeat Ford."

The fellow went into a ten-minute dissertation on all the methods of voter registration, slogans, campaign tactics, and advertising they would be using. Toward the end he asked if we were from the area.

"No, Washington," we replied.

He paled slightly. "Are you in government?"

"The White House," we said unblinkingly.

He looked stricken. We left him with his entourage. Our Dole tour of the state fair was uneventful except for the local announcer who would not shut up. He enthusiastically welcomed Dole, saying, "Here's a man who is not afraid to get out in that barnyard . . . yes folks, he's got dirt on his feet. That's what we need in Washington, more politicians with dirt on their feet." The crowd was chuckling at Dole's obvious discomfort.

On our way out the announcer exclaimed, "Come on over here, senator, I want to shake your hand. I shook with Nixon, you know."

Everyone howled.

On October 15, the vice presidential debate pitted Dole against his opponent, Walter Mondale. The even-handed and respectful debate was overshadowed by Dole's assertion that Democrats had started all the wars in the twentieth century. A press brouhaha followed. Dole was labeled a "hatchet man," an impression that would follow us the rest of the campaign. Surprisingly, the television appearance immediately boosted interest in our visits; cities were added to our itinerary. Advances became two days.

I found myself back in the Midwest for the final stretch of the 1976 race. While the controversies may have colored Dole's image, they seemed to energize the crowds. The turnout was larger. We inched up in the poles. I barnstormed through Illinois, Missouri, and Oklahoma, passing two-dozen times through O'Hare Airport. Someone told me later that we went to thirty-five cities in the last ten days of the campaign.

I rejoined Pam Laudenslager, who had acquired a new site advance, Sherrie Marshall, a young law student from North Carolina. A small and soft-spoken Southern belle, Sherrie was quietly a steel magnolia in the making. An unusually diligent worker, Sherrie became famous for mastering every detail, and her warm Southern personality made our assignments together a pleasure. The team meshed as we ricocheted around Middle America in the campaign's last weeks.

We produced a rally in the Waterloo Civic Center and a speech in "Soy Bean Capital," Hudson, Iowa. While we were still basking in the glow of several good events in a row, Sherrie got a call from Larry Eastland, one of our campaign managers. The staff room went quiet as Pam and I listened. From her end of the conversation, it was clear that Eastland was trying to send her to another team. "But I want to stay with Terry and Pam," she insisted. We wildly waved thumbs-up at her. "Well," she said after listening for long minutes, "if I can't stay with my team, maybe I should go back to school. I'm already missing the beginning of the semester . . ." We shook our fists encouragingly. The steel was starting to show.

She finally hung up, slumping dejectedly. We went into a group hug. After a few seconds of torturing us, Sherrie smiled and said, "He said I could stay." She screamed and jumped into Pam's arms.

"Where were they sending you?" Pam asked.

"They wanted to put me with the president for the last week."

Less than two hours later, Doug Blaser called for me. "I promised I would get you with the president, so we're sending you out West for the last week."

Of course I wanted to be on presidential stops, but how could I abandon Pam and Sherrie when Sherrie had just made her difficult sacrifice. "Doug, I appreciate that you remembered, but we have a smoothly functioning machine here, and I don't want to throw sand in the gears."

For once he didn't sound disappointed in me. "Okay. I've been hearing good things. Keep it up."

* * *

Our final trip for the Dole campaign was a RON (Remain Over Night) in Texas. *An overnight! Double the trouble.*

Midland and Odessa, Texas, are twin cities in the heart of oil country. It became obvious as we met with the GOP locals that there was a distinct chill in the air. While both towns, only fifteen miles apart, are staunchly Republican, the local party establishment from Midland cannot get along with the GOP committee in Odessa. They were together for our meeting, but the Odessa faction was clearly miffed that Dole was coming to Midland. Our principal host, Jimmy Allison, the local newspaper publisher, warned us not to expect much help from Odessa. "But *we* will more than make up for it," he promised.

And he did. Jimmy and his wife, Linda, spent every waking hour over the next several days smoothing the way for us.

On my first night, David Wendell called with a crisis. "Baxter, more important than the stop, more important than Dole, is the laundry."

"Laundry. What laundry?"

"*Our* laundry. We haven't had a stop in a week that was long enough to get any laundry or dry cleaning done. Everyone is starting to smell a little second-hand. You *have* to get the laundry done." He signed off.

Now I was on the hot seat. The plane was arriving late Saturday night and leaving Sunday morning after an airport rally. Where in the world would I get laundry and dry cleaning for sixty people done overnight on a Saturday/Sunday in a one-horse Texas town? My head spun all night.

We were staying at the Midland Hilton. I met first thing with the manager. He just shook his head. No laundry service on the weekend. I asked him to call his cleaning service. He said he would, but could make no promises.

I went through the yellow pages with no success. I tried the hotel in Odessa—no weekend laundry. I was flirting with desperation. I could see Terry, Pam, and Sherrie at the coin-operated Laundromat, except there wasn't one.

I told the Allisons my sad tale. Linda disappeared to make a phone call and returned with a triumphant smile. "The company who supplies our industrial rags at the printing plant will put on an overnight crew to do laundry. Sorry, no dry cleaning, but at least they can renew their underwear."

I kissed her hand. Saved by the industrial rag company. Perhaps I wouldn't reveal that detail. I told David "laundry but no dry cleaning" and he sounded relieved.

We labeled laundry bags for each staff and press person arriving, and entered instructions in the schedule for everyone to deposit their laundry in the press room by midnight. Since it was everyone's last stop for the campaign, we planned a Halloween party for the press and staff in the hotel lounge, hosted, after some schmoozing, by Jimmy and Linda Allison. We also persuaded Leddy's Boot and Saddle Shop to open for two hours Sunday morning for anyone who wanted a custom Stetson or boots. Both were big hits.

The pride of the fourth estate stumbled out of the airplane at 10:00 p.m. looking worse than they smelled. But their spirits were high. Gerald Ford's pole numbers now matched Carter's. The election was being billed as a toss-up. The press, who had often been surly and dismissive, were now suddenly our best friends. They were pinching each other at the prospect of becoming a White House correspondent.

The October 31 headline in the *Washington Star* was "Dole Suddenly Believes: He Might Be the Veep." Word circulated that John Connally, once a Democrat who was struck by the assassin's bullet that passed through John F. Kennedy in Dallas, called Dole to "guarantee" that the Republicans would carry Texas, and thereby win the election. The atmosphere at our impromptu Halloween party was jubilant.

The Halloween drinks flowed, the laundry was all collected, and the last rally of our campaign was after church the next morning. What could go wrong?

\* \* \*

I stumbled to the press room Sunday morning, my head pounding, to check on the laundry. Just as I arrived, they wheeled in a large fabric cart loaded with clothes. The terrible realization finally penetrated my fuzzy brain: *all of the clothes were together in one undifferentiated bin. Heaven help me.*

"I'm sorry," said the man from the commercial laundry, "we didn't have time to sort them back into the individual bags. I'm sure people will be able to identify their own belongings . . ."

Before I had time to enjoy my heart attack, pressies began showing up in hotel robes to claim their underwear. I quickly organized a U-shape of tables and laid out the clothes in small clumps. The T-shirts were neatly folded, the unmentionables smelled sweet and fresh, the socks were matched in little balls, but it seemed impossible that a major eruption of indignation could be averted. Of course, David Wendell chose this moment to enter the room in his robe. He simply broke out laughing. "Oh, this is rich," he said.

Without missing a beat, clothes-seekers began circling the tables, retrieving their undies, shirts, and slacks. Good-natured laughter filled the room. Someone held up Jockey shorts emblazoned with little Mickey Mouses (Mickey mice?). "Has Sam Donaldson been here yet? These look like his."

A press woman claimed her pink bra and lacey panties to appreciative aahs from her colleagues. "Wow, Margaret. Who knew?" Others just grabbed and ran. As I watched in amazement, the entire load of clothing was reduced to a manageable remainder in just fifteen minutes. Not a single discouraging word. In the end, every item found an owner except two heavily padded bras, which became the subject of endless speculation on the press plane home.

We next dragged our hangovers to Leddy's Boot and Saddle Shop. Press and staff were treated to a comic routine from the hat shaper who sized up each victim and loudly proclaimed him either a "tinhorn" or a "potential cowboy," or "all hat and no cattle." Some ranked low enough to be "citified Yankee dude ranchers." Robert Owen, Dole's campaign manager, Larry Speakes, our press secretary, David Wendel, and a half-dozen lions of the press corps all weathered the insults to have hats shaped and the brims cut. Several also bought custom boots. We left looking like a happy group of Eastern tourists.

All at once it was out to the airport for our last farewell. We held a rally in an airport hangar. The crowd was only medium sized, but vocal and enthusiastic. Sherrie had a country-and-western band, which had sounded anemic in our rehearsal, but when they started swinging out with "Deep in the Heart of Texas," the crowd began screaming and dancing. The sound echoed inside the hangar to impressive levels. Dole chuckled in delight.

I must say the euphoria even affected me. I was beginning to believe that we had a glimmer of a chance. Dole surprised everyone by pausing at the foot of the ramp to organize a team photo under the wing of the campaign plane. Crew, press, staff, and the candidate smiled like one big happy family.

As the plane lifted off, we were left with our exhaustion. Jimmy and Linda perked us up by taking us home for a Texas barbeque. Afterwards, Jimmy took us to the airport where we exchanged hugs and thanks, and then we boarded our plane in our tourist Stetsons. We slept with our hats on our faces.

I went to work at 6:30 a.m. the next morning to move the (pretend) storage boxes out of my office.

\* \* \*

Dann Stringer and I both had sailboats on the Chesapeake Bay and spent the next decade meeting up to anchor with friends in quiet coves to grill steaks.

Pam Laudenslager became a senior executive for Avon Products and later a two-time Tony, Drama Desk, and Drama League Award-winning Broadway producer. Way to go, Pam.

Sherrie Marshall joined the White House staff in the Reagan administration as associate council and was a commissioner of the Federal Communications Commission from 1989 to 1993.

# 1976 FINALE

The main ballroom was already packed with partiers, so I went in search of the staff rooms. I found a large press room almost completely deserted but well appointed with phones, television sets, and refreshments. I found the main cluster of press advance staff and we began circulating as a group among the hospitality suites. Everywhere the mood was tense, even though no returns had been announced yet.

Then, one after another, the Southern returns were announced, going solidly Carter. We passed through the Dole hospitality suite, meeting some spouses, but it was quiet and stifling. Most revelers had a grim set to their jaws, but several big states were still "too close to call." Diehards continued to hope.

Then, nearing midnight, it was simultaneously announced that both New York and Texas had been declared for Carter. So much for John Connally's guarantee . . .

That was enough for me. I went home to Pat. The last entry in my journal from the 1976 election was, "I'm not sure the best man won, but maybe. I'm willing to hope Jimmy Carter has the potential to be great. That would not only be good for the country, the American people, and the world, but it would forever underscore my memories from 1976."

In the end my hopes were dashed. Carter's presidency was a calamitous mélange of inept policies, micromanagement, malaise, and Iranian hostages. David Broder wrote an insightful appreciation of Gerald Ford in the *Washington Star* on January 16, 1977, the day Carter was inaugurated:

> In an odd, inexplicable way, the truth has begun to dawn on people in the final days of Gerald R. Ford's tenure that he was the kind of President Americans wanted—and didn't know they had.
>
> After a decade of presidential excess, they wanted a man of modesty, good character, honesty and openness. They wanted a President who was humane and prudent, peaceable but firm. Especially, they wanted one uncorrupted by the cynicism and lust for power that they had come to associate with Washington politicians . . . Gerald Ford can leave office with some confidence that history will record that he was, in truth, the President the country needed.

\* \* \*

Jimmy Carter won by 50.1 percent. The twenty-seven states carried by Ford/Dole were the most states ever carried by a losing candidate. Ford lost Texas by 3.2 percent.

Bob Dole went on to become the majority leader of the senate, and ran as the Republican nominee for president in 1996, losing to Bill Clinton. He was later the spokesman for ED, erectile dysfunction.

In the weeks following the election, I received gracious letters from Gerald Ford, Ron Nessen, James Baker, Doug Blaser, Larry Speakes, Steve Studdert, and David Wendell. I never heard from Bob Dole.

# The Years Between the Wars

While it may have felt like I'd been gone a year, it was actually only a couple of months. The sudden end of the campaign left me with an undeniable emptiness at first, but GEICO was in the midst of a concerted effort to emerge from a difficult financial crisis, which culminated in the months after I returned. The rescue required efforts on multiple fronts, and I plunged right into the fray.

Once again, I worked closely with Jack Byrne as he addressed each issue and gradually prevailed. The year that followed brought wrenching changes to the company. GEICO went from a bloated, entrenched bureaucracy to a lean, bottom-line-oriented meritocracy. It emerged smaller, better capitalized, and more focused. Management changed, culture changed, and little by little GEICO returned to an auto insurance powerhouse. The entire experience was the business version of an extreme makeover. It was an exhilarating education.

As the financial and business challenges began to recede, Jack renewed his insistence that GEICO employees be "good corporate citizens," actively involved in community events and charitable, cultural, and political endeavors. As we threw our efforts into such organizations as the International Special Olympics, the National Symphony Orchestra, and the

Children's Hospital, employees found a new esprit de corps. We were also encouraged to take a more active role in industry-related issues like drunk driving and highway safety, which led to relationships with the National Safety Council, The Highway Users Federation, and Mothers Against Drunk Driving. I found the years that followed challenging and satisfying. I became an officer of GEICO (assistant vice president) in 1977, and a vice president in 1980. My mother's bridge club was exhilarated.

*  *  *

As the presidential election year of 1980 approached, I was deluged with calls from my former political colleagues. The bugle was sounding; the musketeers were assembling. "Who are you planning to go with in the primaries?" was the standard question. I equivocated. The siren call was hard to resist, but with my new responsibilities at GEICO, I couldn't afford another four-month campaign break, so I watched with interest, but no participation, as the primaries heated up on both sides.

Jimmy Carter faced a serious challenge from Edward Kennedy, along with boomlets from Jerry Brown and Edmund Muskie. The Republican primaries were a free for all between Ronald Reagan, George H. W. Bush, John Anderson, Howard Baker, John Connally, and Bob Dole.

I watched the emergence of Ronald Reagan as a candidate for the Republican nomination with pleasure and excitement. If I'd had any inside connections in the Reagan campaign, I would have been sorely tempted, but most of the calls I got were from Bush, Baker, or Dole operatives. I had no idea how to reach Bob Tuttle, or even if he was involved again with Reagan. The era of the internet would have simplified things immensely, but it was a decade away.

After Reagan won the nomination, I was finally tracked down by one of my former volunteers who had been working with the Reagan campaign. I agreed to a one-week tour of the Midwest with a "truth squad," a small team of surrogates to counter Carter campaign claims. My VIPs were Elizabeth Dole (I was pleased when she greeted me warmly) and William Simon. We had our own little Learjet, which flitted from town to Midwest town where I did my best each time to assemble a small press conference for our panel. We were a sideshow to the campaign. The press were jaded and uninterested. It really was dog duty, but it was only a week.

To my delight, Reagan won in a landslide. I could return to GEICO with the glow of being part of the winning side, however small my role had been.

At long last Bob Tuttle reemerged. When he got to Washington, he remembered to look for me at GEICO. We had dinner to celebrate the election. Bob revealed that he was heading the main inaugural event before the swearing-in, "The Governor's Reception," where President-elect Reagan would host his fellow governors in the ballroom of a Washington hotel. Before the night was over, I became Tuttle's deputy for the event.

Austin Kiplinger, who I knew from the National Symphony Orchestra, was chairman of the Governor's Reception, so we had organizational star power. We put the event together over several weeks of evening work, and I recruited a small team of GEICO executives to be part of our tuxedoed "men in black" advance squad.

The Governor's Reception was a fine success. My GEICO colleagues were effusive with their thanks. Afterwards, the Inaugural Committee reserved us a block of rooms in the hotel so we, along with our spouses, could party late into the night without the risk of impaired driving—GEICO's safety consciousness in action.

Groggily, we shared a room-service brunch the next morning in the staff room, and proudly watched Reagan's inaugural address. His swearing in was cross-cut on television with the emotional release of the Iranian hostages as he spoke. All moments we will long remember.

Flush with the excitement of a new president I admired, I asked GEICO if I could begin to bank all of my vacation for the next several years so I could participate in the next election cycle. Perhaps because four years seemed a long way off, my bosses agreed.

\* \* \*

The attempt on Ronald Reagan's life in March 1981 was suddenly more personal because this was *my* president. The two attempts to shoot Gerald Ford were just before my tenure in 1976. (In September 1975, Lynette "Squeaky" Fromme, a Charles Manson follower, was tackled by the Secret Service before she could act. Seventeen days later, Sarah Jane Moore fired a shot before she was also subdued.)

Jimmy Carter faced his own rendezvous with destiny in 1979 when attacked by a "killer rabbit." Carter reported the brute was "hissing menacingly, teeth flashing, nostrils flared."

The *Sarasota Herald Tribune* summarized it this way:

A "killer rabbit" attacked President Carter on a recent trip to Plains, Georgia, penetrating Secret Service security and forcing the Chief Executive to beat back the beast with a canoe paddle.

An Associated Press writer called it "a metaphor for Carter's hapless, enfeebled presidency."

President Reagan's assault by John Hinckley was the most serious. Reagan was shot outside a Washington hotel where he had just delivered a speech. His press secretary, a Washington policeman, and a Secret Service agent were also seriously injured.

In the midst of the chaos, the White House lead, Rick Ahearn, and Secret Service agent-in-charge, Jerry Parr, coolly initiated an immediate departure of the president's car. Parr initially directed the presidential limo ("Stagecoach") to return to "Crown" (the White House). But when Parr noticed frothy blood on Reagan's lips, he redirected the car to George Washington University Hospital. They arrived in four minutes.

Still on the scene of the attack, Rick Ahearn hovered over press secretary James Brady, who was critically wounded in the head. Rick maintained pressure on the seeping wound until Brady was loaded into an ambulance. Ahearn and Secret Service agent Jim Varey leaped in to accompany their stricken colleague. "George Washington University Hospital," Rick shouted.

"No can do," the ambulance driver replied. "I have to return to the hospital that dispatched me."

Jim Varey leaned over the back of the driver's seat. "Listen very carefully. Get us to George Washington ASAP. Do it now."

The driver considered the demeanor of the armed Secret Service agent and decided that GW was a good choice. The short distance to the hospital was vital to Brady's subsequent survival.

Reagan lost half his blood. In shock, he came close to death, but his sense of humor never left him. He told one of his aides, "I'd rather be here than Philadelphia" (W. C. Fields' famous epitaph). Just before surgery, Reagan took off his oxygen mask to address the assembled doctors, "I hope you are all Republicans."

Dr. Giordano, a staunch Democrat, said, "Today, Mr. President, we are *all* Republicans."

When Nancy Reagan reached the recovery room, Reagan told her, "Honey, I forgot to duck."

These events would have a game-changing impact on presidential campaigns. The Secret Service quite sensibly introduced a requirement that all attendees at presidential events, including campaign events, submit to screening for weapons. Background checks became more intensive. Metal detectors (magnetometers, or "mags") became a new feature of advance work. And, just like airport security, the additional screening slowed the crowds dramatically. Event planning now required early arrival incentives like entertainment, and an increasing burden on secret service technicians, budgets, and advance teams.

\* \* \*

In 1982, Jack Byrne agreed to be the chairman of a fund-raising movie premiere for the Special Olympics, which included lunch under a tent on the South Lawn of the White House. I spent all afternoon the day before the event checking the seating arrangements to make sure Jack and Dorothy Byrne would be close to the president. The White House social secretary and a Washington party planner were constantly rearranging the tables. Each time, I would scrutinize the Byrnes' tablemates. Eunice and Sarge Shriver were always with them, along with two seats marked Potus, and a changing array of other dignitaries.

After one break, I came back to find the Byrne table on the other side of the room. Aside from the Shrivers and the Potuses, the table's dignitaries were all rearranged again. Worried that I was getting rolled, I asked, "Isn't this farther away from the president?"

Amused, the social secretary pointed to the seating chart of the Byrne table. "POTUS," she declared, "President Of The United States."

"Oh," I said laughing at myself. I pointed, "I assumed the president was on the platform marked here."

"No, that's where the Beach Boys will perform. We didn't think you'd want to be so close to the music."

I had been in and out of the White House for years and had never heard the term POTUS. *How to feel like a rookie in one easy lesson.* "Thanks," I said nodding and laughing again. "I'm sure I'll be safe in your hands." Washington had become a blizzard of acronyms: POTUS, FLOTUS (First Lady), SCOTUS (Supreme Court), OMB (Office of Management and Budget, which had PADs, Program Associate Directors, and DADs, Deputy Associate Directors), NSC, NSA, RNC, PACs, and eventually "ED" and "low T." *It's a new world.*

* * *

It's hard to believe it would take another accidental encounter to bring me into the Reagan campaign team, but it did. I met Ron Walker at a cocktail reception in Don Regan's home. Walker assumed from my presence that I worked in the administration. "No," I said, "but I did some advance work." An impressive former Army Ranger, Walker went on to explain that he had been the first director of White House advance when it was newly established in the Nixon White House. Ron Walker literally wrote the manual on advance work. He went on to professionalize the practices that had been mostly ad hoc. Doug Blaser was one of his best friends. We passed a happy cocktail hour swapping stories.

When the Reagan team was casting a net to recruit advancemen for the 1984 campaign, Ron Walker passed along my name. The advance seminar was in early December 1983, a Friday–Saturday–Sunday affair. The leadoff was a very nice reception and dinner Friday night at the Capitol Hill Club. It was great to see Steve Studdert and Ron Walker participating.

The seminar was all day Saturday at the Mayflower Hotel, and a half day on Sunday. Welcoming remarks were from Bill Henkel, the director of White House advance for Reagan, Mike Deaver, the deputy chief of staff, and RNC chairman Frank Fahrenkopf.

Mike McManus, Deaver's deputy, quickly put our role in perspective. "When I first went out on an advance, I thought maybe the president wanted to talk to me about political strategy or world events. I ended up painting signs."

But Deaver himself was more lyrical and said, "If you become a lead, you are the personal representative of the President of the United States." *That* lingered in my mind.

We received a series of briefings from the military aides, WHCA, Air Force One—"We strive for an equal number of takeoffs and landings"—the United States Secret Service, and the counsel's office on legal guidelines (presented by Sherrie Marshall, now Cooksey, associate counsel to the president).

Sunday's sessions covered press advance and a panel discussion on press considerations from representatives of NBC, ABC, CBS, CNN, and AP. Susan Zirinsky (CBS) summarized, "Let's be honest, if it's not on the network, it didn't really happen."

Henkel finished with, "Advance work is what *makes* a campaign. It's now up to you. I promise you, you will come away with some of the most enduring friendships you will ever make. Clear your calendars. We will try to schedule you for a presidential trip in the next month or two."

Mine came in February.

# Viva Las Vegas

February 1984

I met Mark Hatfield on the airplane en route to Las Vegas. He was an unforgettable character. The young and handsome son of a prominent senator, he had worked with the Reagan family since he was a teenager. He was high-energy and had irrepressible wit. His expressions were endlessly animated. Relating a tale, his eyebrows crawled up to his hairline, his eyes danced with glee, and his smile was mischievously exuberant, as though he couldn't hide the little boy that lived inside.

Hatfield would be the lead press advance for the fundraiser we were arranging in Las Vegas. I had crossed over from "press" to "staff" responsibilities. We had a four-day head start over the president's arrival. I was to advance the hotel, which would be RON (remain overnight) for the president's party. RON trips entailed endless detail work, starting with room assignments for the president's immediate party and the traveling staff. For RONs, WHCA rewired the entire hotel to provide each room with a White House telephone, or "drops" (in addition to the normal hotel phone). Drops had no dial tone. When picked up, a WHCA operator immediately answered, "Las Vegas Signal," or, once Air Force One had landed, "Las Vegas White House," a reminder that you enjoyed all the resources of the White House communications center. If your extension was "110" in the White House, then your extension in the hotel would be "110." Signal could instantly connect you to anyone, ranging from the White House switchboard to a secure line at the Pentagon. If your party did not answer his drop, signal could locate him through a network of pagers, advising him to "Two-two" (call) the board.

I had little time to ponder this as Hatfield filled the flight from Washington with war stories and hilarious imitations of Walt McCay, the colorful Texan who was to be our lead.

"He makes his arm into 'Big Boy,'" Mark said demonstrating. His forearm rose from his lap like a hooded cobra. His hand was in a fist, wrist cocked forward and swiveling like a small head. "Big Boy's aroused," Mark said, adopting McCay's Texas accent. "Loooooking, always looooking." The Wang girl (White House computer operator) traveling with us shied away across the aisle. Big Boy instantly zeroed in on her movement. Her eyes grew wide with feigned horror. "Target sighted," Hatfield chortled.

I had been warned to try to keep a lid on Hatfield and McCay after their antics had caused a stir on an earlier stop. I was only beginning to understand. Hatfield went on to relate McCay's reputed fortune from ranching interlaced with Tex-Mex parodies of McCay's jokes.

"If he dies on this trip, I get his watch," Hatfield said just as we were landing. Thus primed, the first thing I noticed about the dapper lead with an Errol Flynn mustache was his huge Rolex. He wore an expensively tailored suit, a little sharp perhaps, had a honeyed voice, and an expanse of white teeth as big as Texas when he smiled. He took my hand in both of his and said, "You must be Baxter. I've heard a lot about you. Welcome to the team." I felt like he was the veteran CO welcoming the rookie airman to the squadron. It felt good.

Mark and Walt wrapped each other in an enormous bear hug. The chemistry between them was obviously longstanding. I could see I had my work cut out to fit in.

In the staff office, we had two elderly women from the local party to man our phones. They fussed over us like mother hens. Their devotion was tested on the very first day. Hatfield got a call from a volunteer on a previous stop. She wanted to come to Las Vegas. Hatfield immediately agreed to personally pay for her flight. As he hung up, he levitated off the chair.

"Linda is on her way," Hatfield exulted, his voice a fever pitch. "Put her in the room with the sauna," he said to me, the "hotel guy."

Hatfield and McCay proceeded to dance around the room in giddy celebration. It gradually emerged that the lovely Linda was the younger sister of the most fearsome linebacker in the NFL. While this did not seem to cool Mark or Walt's ardor, I had visions of him crashing into the room in a rage as Hatfield and McCay ever more gleefully one-upped each other in describing the sexual positions they planned for her.

My concern for the delicate sensibilities of our two listening grandmothers ebbed as I watched them nudge each other and begin to laugh uncontrollably as the demonstration grew. They were limp and tear-stained by the time McCay and Hatfield finally calmed down.

Linda arrived later in the day to surprisingly appropriate decorum from our boys.

She was indeed beautiful, and tiny. It was hard to imagine her brother as the ferocious football star, who was, well, not beautiful. She was as efficient as she was attractive; she jumped right into the trip preparations like an old hand.

Our first order of business, as always, was the schedule. The president's schedule is the bible of a visit. Every day is detailed in five-minute increments, starting with the president's departure from the White House. Our part was from the point of arrival in Las Vegas: who would greet him at the airport, who would ride in what vehicle, seating on the speech platform, introductions, and movements at each site, with diagrams of all locations showing movements of the president, press, and staff with different symbols. There were manifests for Air Force One, manifests for each vehicle in the motorcade, even manifests for which elevator to occupy. Walt and I would consult each day with the White House Advance Office, the White House Press Office, and sometimes with the senior staff, to fill in the details day by day until a final schedule was distributed to participants.

The emerging schedule was the focal point for our countdown meetings at the end of each day. The major participants of the visit, along with WHCA and the Secret Service, would hash through any problems the planned events or movements created. It was a process of constant change and constant refinement. The early countdowns could extend for several hours as many of the details were confronted for the first time. The meetings got progressively shorter as the event approached. Afterwards, the advance team usually went to dinner as a group. Each night was a riot of Walt's jokes, interspersed with appearances from Big Boy. Walt's politically incorrect jokes were related in tones as rich as Corinthian leather. His genuine good nature precluded any offense. Hatfield and McCay tried to top each other with outlandish stories of previous trips. Was it off the wall? Frequently. Was it ever boring? Never. Eventually, I would come to think of Mark Hatfield as the brother I never had, and Walt McCay, nearly so.

It was our third countdown meeting where my welcome to the advance team became a hazing ritual. After the Ford campaign, I had written a suspense thriller, *Hailstone*. It came out at the end of 1983. (It's an incredibly riveting book still available from the out-of-print bookshop at Amazon; although, it is hard to believe anyone is willing to part with it.) In *Hailstone*, (spoiler alert) the villain is a rogue Secret Service agent. Unknown to me, *Hailstone* was on sale in the hotel gift shop. One of our agents for the trip stumbled across it, and shared it with his entire team. They began to scheme a payback.

The night of our third countdown, we had a full table: the mayor, the hotel manager, the chief of police, WHCA, four Secret Service agents, and our advance team. We were covering some mundane business when the lead Secret Service agent suddenly interjected, "She remembered the night, lying in front of the fire, and the boy with the smiling eyes . . ."

The room fell silent, trying to understand the strange interruption. The agent gave nothing away with his expression. I started to realize there was something vaguely familiar about the words.

Then the agent across the room spoke up, "She undid her blouse with trembling fingers . . ." Then it hit me. They were reciting lines from my sex scene in *Hailstone*.

I started laughing. Several others smiled, not understanding why.

Then the third agent recited the next, more lurid, excerpt. I was overcome with guffaws. Others started laughing with me. I had already suffered from exaggerated parodies of my novel's scenes from my GEICO co-workers. Now, the Secret Service was skewering me with exact quotes. My countdown colleagues laughed louder with each incongruous statement; they knew something very funny was happening, but they couldn't fathom what.

Finally, mercifully, the last agent, who was trying hard not to smirk, quoted the last line, and everyone in the room roared. When the pandemonium subsided, the agents huddled around me to explain to the others that *I* was the source of the purple prose. "From now on, Baxter, remember, agents are *the good guys*," the Secret Service lead concluded, clapping me on the shoulder.


The rest of the trip was a breeze. You already know about Walt's rendezvous with Miss Springtime and the president's "surprise" birthday celebration. The fundraiser was a huge success. No NFL linebacker attacked us with the intention of inflicting great bodily harm.

I had survived my Reagan initiation.

As is frequently the case, when not much news accompanies a trip, the press tends to focus on nitpicking. This time there were comments about the apparent presence of stewardesses in Hatfield's press area. *Quelle horreur!* There was also an "exposé" about our wheels-up party hosted by the hotel. "Las Vegas show girls wall to wall," was one description. "Cheap skates," was another charge leveled. We had simply accepted the hotel's invitation to a "little celebration." We had no role in any of the arrangements. The hotel picked up the tab and paid the staff. When we pooled our ready cash to add to the tip for the servers, the result was derided as "trickle-down economics."

Washington shrugged it off as one more McCay and Hatfield antic.

\* \* \*

Shortly after Las Vegas, I learned I was included for the state visit to China in the late spring. To prepare for this major thrill, I decided to upgrade my radio earpiece.

The WHCA radios of 1984 were a big step up from our original Motorolas, but we still called them "bricks." The units issued to volunteers had little circular earpieces held loosely in the ear by a wire clip. This worked reasonably well on the lead-up to the event, since the noise level was manageable. But once the bands started and the crowd cheered, you were suddenly deaf, with all chance of coordination at the site ruined. The permanent staff, Secret Service, WHCA, and nearly all leads invested in molded earpieces, where a model of the ear canal was taken to produce a silicone insert. This effectively sealed out ambient noise, and, more importantly, distinguished you from mere volunteers sporting the little round ear clips.

\* \* \*

My first surprise on the China trip was a pleasant one: my old classmate from the University of Maryland, Mark Rosenker, was the press advance. We had been television students together at the University of Maryland. We enjoyed getting reacquainted. The next surprise was not so happy: our lead for the trip was the only lead I ever worked with that I concluded was not up to the demands of the job. Since he possessed a passing resemblance to Colonel Klink from the old TV show *Hogan's Heroes*, I will call him "Klink."

Klink had a grating voice and a sour disposition. When he was angry, his jowls flapped like Richard Nixon's. His loose-limbed movements reminded me of Howdy Doody without the smile. His control of events was tenuous. He often lost his temper, screaming and flailing his arms like he was trying to take off, and every mistake was someone else's fault.

While Klink's leadership did not engender much fun, we worked hard to cover his lapses, and the trip was a historic success. At another China stop, Hatfield and McCay reportedly caused some headscratching among the Chinese, but even this was forgotten in the general good feelings of the aftermath.

The food will be a lingering memory. The sweet people hosting us prepared one specialty every day at noon. We were on our own for dinner. Each mid-day plate arrived with a folded sheet of paper, a Chinese symbol on the front, and the "English" translation on the inside.

The Cantonese say, "anything that walks, swims, crawls, or flies with its back to heaven is edible." We were certain our hosts were testing this theory on us. The first day, they brought us our plates and little menus, then withdrew to the kitchen as if to escape.

The translation read, "Black fungus soup." We tasted cautiously. Ah, mushroom soup. Good too. We joked that our hosts were peeking at us, asking each other, "Did they eat it?" like "Mikey" in the TV commercial.

"Yeah."

"Okay, wait until tomorrow!"

Each day, they seemed to up the ante: camel hump stew, dragon meat (snake; cobra is "five-step" snake—take five steps before you die), bird's nest soup, and stinky tofu (*chou dofu*; some Chinese vendors of this "taste treat" have been cited for air pollution).

On the last day, each plate was covered with a little dome. Chinese character on the front, translation inside said, "Crap Patty."

One in our party said, "I've eaten black fungus, camel hump, bird's nest, and snake, but I draw the line at eating crap."

We removed our domes to find, of course, a perfectly delicious crab cake.

# "God Bless the USA"

Our trip to Decatur, Illinois, was to be the last fundraiser before the Republican Convention in Dallas. It would finish with an airport rally before departure. My lead was Grey Terry, one of the permanent White House advancemen (along with Jim Hooley, Rick Ahearn, and Andrew Littlefair). I felt it was a vote of confidence to work the site directly under such an experienced White House hand.

Grey Terry was a mature former longtime General Motors executive. His calm confidence was a welcome change from Klink. Grey was wiry and had more hair than should be legal. He talked out of the side of his mouth and had a way of scrunching his eyes when he spoke, which Jim Hooley, our campaign leader, could parody perfectly—two seconds and you knew it was Grey Terry.

In Illinois, we were backed up by a good local team, a jovial regional coordinator, and a crackerjack office manager, Charlie. Mike Brennan, a personable Californian, would do the fundraising site; I would do the airport rally.

Decatur was where I first began to appreciate the transforming effect of bleachers. My site was the bare airport tarmac featuring nothing but asphalt and a chain-link fence. Even a sizable crowd would be dwarfed by the wide-open spaces. At our first meeting with the locals, I asked about getting bleachers. They looked at each other with blank expressions. Moving bleachers? That would be Herculean.

I began to see an event arc that repeated itself over and over: I would fly into a strange town, usually late in the day. I would have arranged to meet with a group of volunteers from the local party at, say, 9:00 p.m., already an inconvenience to them. I would introduce myself, and say something like, "The President of the United States is coming to Smallville in three days. We will need platforms, bunting, bands, and, oh, we'll have to move the bleachers from the football stadium to the town square."

They would think to themselves, *what an asshole.* One-third would never return, but some new people would show up the next day, and ideas would start to emerge on how to accomplish the impossible. Wonderful and creative helpers would pitch in, the American way in action.

On the third day, platforms would appear, bleachers would start to arrive, and the surviving volunteers high-fived each other and congratulated themselves on what they had accomplished. I would start to be smarter than I used to be.

On the fourth day, the crowds would surge, the president would arrive, the bands would play, and I was suddenly a great guy. Euphoria reigned. The locals would want me to marry their daughters. But, alas, I would fly off to another new city to meet with a new group of volunteers late at night, and they would say to themselves, *what an asshole.*

Three days as an asshole, and one day as a potential bridegroom. What a life.

Advancemen are by and large type A personalities with no shortage of ego. I had a high regard for duty, honor, and total commitment. I was vaguely aware that I had an overdeveloped single-mindedness. I had been a television director and race car driver, schooled in rapid-fire decision making. It was relatively easy to convince myself that whatever I was doing at the moment was the most important mission on the planet. But, to paraphrase Fess Parker as Davy Crockett, "Be sure you're right, then press ahead." Or, as Winston Churchill said, even closer to my own code, "It is not enough to say we did our best. We must succeed in doing what is necessary."

Too demanding? Sometimes, no doubt. I tried to temper my insistence, but I was loath to compromise an event. We started with an incredible advantage—a *great* candidate. Now we needed an event that matched. My volunteers seemed to take this in stride, and I am comforted by the many friendships that continued for years later. I know we left many happy memories and good feelings in our wake.

So, with no apologies, bleachers became one of my standard tricks. With bleachers forming the horizon behind a crowd, the sea of faces appeared to go on forever. I later augmented this effect by placing a second set of bleachers on flatbed trucks behind the first row. This created a stadium out of a flat lot.

The crowd looked much larger than a group of people standing shoulder to shoulder. It gave the site texture.

For Decatur, the four single sets of bleachers nicely framed the standing masses in the middle. Then another happy suggestion bubbled up from my volunteers: one of the high schools had a renowned choir. I went to listen to them; they were great. I invited them to perform for the president, and they agreed.

The kids were all attractive and harmonized beautifully. One young man, a large black student, had a strong, clear voice. I asked the choir director if he could do a solo.

"He does all the time," she said. We started looking through her sheet music to pick a song. Right on top was Lee Greenwood's new country hit, "God Bless the USA."

I had already heard it and loved it.

The day before the president's arrival, I knew we had a large crowd on our hands when over a thousand people lined the chain-link fence just to watch the limo planes land (US military transports carrying the presidential limousine, podium, and teams of Secret Service agents). A team of our huskiest volunteers nudged the bleachers back ten feet to accommodate more participants. A huge, enthusiastic Decatur audience sent President Reagan off to the Republican Convention with a heartfelt salute. "God Bless the USA" was a magic moment. Mike Deaver ran over to me and snatched the sheet music out of my hand as he rushed for the plane.

* * *

I wish I could remember the name of that young black singer. I would love to know if he is now a professional performer. I hope so. Grey Terry and Mike Brennan continue to be close friends over the long years since Decatur.

# DE ANZA COLLEGE

Over the break following the convention, I received my campaign credential, a laminated photo ID card that read "Advance Representative, THE WHITE HOUSE." My photo looked like I was against the wall before a firing squad, but I can't deny that my chest swelled. I was also finally awarded a permanent enameled staff pin. I finally felt official.

The 1984 campaign began in earnest in California.

For opening day, we were in Cupertino, the heart of Silicon Valley, headquarters for Apple Computer. Our staff office was a large hotel suite filled with eager volunteers. The lead was Jim Hooley, the heir apparent in the White House Advance Office, so we all had good reason to consider ourselves the A Team.

It was an incredible stroke of luck to be paired with Jim Hooley. He went beyond logistics and smooth operations. Jim had a commanding vision for events—color, drama, audience involvement—he was committed to delivering a memorable experience. To his team he was welcoming, inclusive, and tolerant of rookies. But most of all, he was fun. Hooley possessed an ironic personality and a dashing moustache.

His quick wit was combined with a hilarious repertoire of advanceman quirks. With an elastic face, he could instantly evoke Grey Terry's scrunch, or Ron Walker's supercilious countenance. He puffed up his chest and lowered his voice to become Rick Ahearn's pedantic Boston Brahman. Hooley, a natural mimic, also nailed Mark Rosenker's unique laugh— Mark made a sort of squishing noise on the roof of his mouth, which emerged as a sort of "cheeesch, cheeesch, cheeesch."

One day, we will all get together and retaliate with our Jim Hooley imitations. My entry will mimic Jim's hemming and hawing inner diplomat when dealing with event hosts. It will go something like this: (earnest voice) "Do you have a minute, I don't want to interrupt. I wonder if I might make a suggestion? It's a small matter, I don't want to make too much of it. And it's not like the White House is asking for this. It is your event. The decision is entirely yours. You may have already thought of this yourself. And you know the customs of your organization so much better than we do, so don't feel you have to respond right away. This may not be the best idea you've ever heard, but what would you think . . ."

After such interminable foreplay, most listeners were ready to pull out his tongue with pliers. Mark Rosenker, rarely concerned about diplomacy, would have simply said, "Let's move your national sales conference from Milwaukee to Miami—hey, they both start with 'M,' cheeesch, cheesch, cheesch."

My site was a large green on the campus of De Anza College, a 112-acre liberal arts college built on the former grounds of the Beaulieu Vineyard in 1967. De Anza had produced such notables as Steve Wozniak, cofounder of Apple.

We were imagining a Fourth of July celebration without the fireworks, a happy family occasion. We wanted to welcome students and townspeople alike. A key mission was to turn the empty green into a festive arcade, to entertain the audience and add color. "Be creative," we were told. So our volunteers fanned out in search of strolling musicians, facepainters, mimes, hot dog stands, spun-sugar vendors, magicians, and a stilt walker—no idea was rejected out-of-hand, until I proposed skydivers. It became the most contentious impasse of our first countdown meeting.

I pictured three skydivers circling down toward the field, red, white, and blue smoke billowing behind as "God Bless the USA" was performed. (Mike Deaver had sent a notice to all leads requesting that Lee Greenwood's song be included in every campaign stop; I was delighted to have a role in creating our campaign anthem, and even more pleased when I met Lee Greenwood later in the campaign.)

Of course, there were plenty of potential disasters in a skydiving display. One of the jumpers could plummet to the earth in a headline-producing tragedy. Or, one of them could land amid the crowd instead of our landing zone and injure a spectator. In spite of the potential hazards, I could tell Hooley had warmed to my idea.

The Secret Service said, "No way. How would we know who is coming out of the plane?"

"Put an agent in the airplane," I countered.

"We don't have the manpower. The airspace over the site is closed," the lead Secret Service agent insisted. "No skydivers."

This was another example of a familiar campaign story arc: security versus access. The Secret Service had a difficult and vital job: protecting the president. Their preferred campaign scenario would have the president escorted directly to a secure bank vault. Our preferred scenario would have the president wade into the crowd and greet every voter personally. Many of our countdown discussions were about how to accomplish some balance of both missions. Usually we reached compromises and went on to the next issue. But sometimes, often from a lack of sufficient diplomacy, the Secret Service and the advanceman would stand firm on their positions.

Their trump card was to say, "We'll take it to the director of the Presidential Protection Division." That was the assistant director of the Secret Service!

Our trump card was to say, "We'll take it to Mike Deaver." That was the chief of staff to the president!

Of course, neither of us really wanted to advertise our failure to negotiate a compromise. The threats to escalate were usually bluffs, which evaporated over the next twenty-four hours when one side or the other suddenly discovered an accommodation.

On this occasion Hooley simply concluded, "We'll revisit this later. Next issue."

The next day, the staff office was humming. Ever more worker bees materialized. One of the most attractive young volunteers, Shelby Scarbrough, had a connection to a local Mexican restaurant and arranged what must have been a twenty-gallon tub of salsa. Her popularity, already nearly off the scale, soared to new heights.

The office began to resemble *America's Got Talent* try-outs. Amid auditioning jugglers, mimes, and clowns, staffers consumed prodigious quantities of chips and salsa while manning phones, making lists, and placating various audience seekers.

Hooley, Baxter, and Hatfield went off to meet Mayor Plungee, a Democrat with an oily smile, which he displayed at odd moments as if turned on by a remote button. But he was jovial in that artificial political way and offered any assistance to make the president's visit a success. We invited him to join the president on the platform during the rally and he beamed.

At that night's countdown, the lead Secret Service agent began by announcing he had considered the skydivers overnight and was now certain he "could make it happen."

"Thank you," Jim Hooley replied. "Now it's *our* fault if the whole thing goes to hell."

Everyone chuckled and moved to other issues. Hooley only told me later that he had called Deaver without even dangling the threat. The skydivers were a go.

The next day, after the tub of salsa had fermented all night, the entire wing of the hotel housing the staff office smelled like pungent garlic and over-ripe tomatoes. It took all day to air it out. Our clothes smelled of it for days.

D day was a dependable California day, sunny and pleasant. Students and parents swarmed the field to claim a spot near the front. Families brought blankets and picnics. The jugglers and mimes and facepainters and clowns wandered through the crowd spreading cheer. I was in the tiny trailer that served as the site command center. Suddenly, I noticed Mayor Plungee's face on the small television screen. I turned up the sound.

It was a local talk show. The mayor was in mid-rant about the cost of President Reagan's visit to the taxpayers of Cupertino, how the motorcade would disrupt traffic, and overtime pay would be required for numerous city departments. He appeared angry and red in the face. My jaw dropped.

While the mayor was glad-handing us, gushing about the honor it was for Cupertino to host the campaign's opening day, he was grousing behind our backs to score some cheap political points with his constituents. He had attended every countdown meeting and never voiced any objections.

My phone rang. It was Hooley, back at the hotel getting ready to head to the airport for the arrival. His voice was agitated. "Did you see that?" he yelled.

"Yeah, unbelievable."

"What do you think we should do?"

"Stiff him," I said without hesitation.

"Do it."


We had a large tent to shield the motorcade's arrival at the field. A few dignitaries who were invited for a photo-op had gathered. Mayor Plungee arrived with his young son, the huge artificial smile glued to his face. He had a ceremonial key to the city with him. I led him gently away from the other guests.

"Mr. Mayor, I have some bad news," I said. "You are not going to meet the president today." The Rosenker method.

The State Department would never requisition my talents for diplomacy.

"What?" The smile left his face as if wiped off by a hand. "Why?"

"We just watched your television interview. We considered it an insult."

His face clouded with anger.

I tried to soften the blow and said, "I have tickets for you and your son in the VIP section if you would like to . . ." But he had already turned and stormed out.


President Reagan's speech that day was terrific. At the conclusion, a children's choir broke into "God Bless the USA." Partway through, people in the crowd started pointing at the sky. The audience was buzzing. The president looked up. His gaze settled on three tiny specks trailing red, white, and blue smoke. Then their parachutes opened and they spiraled down until, just as the song reached its crescendo, they drifted right over the speaker's platform to touch down behind the stage. Reagan clasped his hands overhead and waved as they slid by. I could breathe again.

\* \* \*

Shelby Scarbrough was such a hit in Cupertino that she was invited to Washington to join the staff. She became protocol officer in the State Department from 1987 to 1989. In the years since, she has become one of Washington's premier events planners. Her company is Practical Protocol.

A couple of weeks after the event, Mike Deaver sent me a clipping from the local Cupertino newspaper. The headline read, "Will President Reagan ever get Cupertino's Key to the City?" The gist of the story was Mayor Plungee's sad tale of being confronted by a "Secret Service agent" who barred him from the rally because he had "embarrassed" the president. Plungee mused that perhaps he would be invited to the White House one day to present the orphaned key to the president. Deaver had scrawled at the bottom of the story, "Don't hold your breath."

# One-Punch Baxter

We were a pretty well-oiled team by the time we rolled into Waterbury, Connecticut. Hooley, Hatfield, and I fell into a natural rhythm of lead, press, and site, and went about our preparations with minimum discussion. Not that there weren't plenty of new lessons.

After the get-to-know-each-other success of Cupertino, we did a quick visit to an IBM facility in upstate New York. It was a large plant with interesting technology on display, and attractive employees eager to greet the president. I had fun with the IBM staff selecting visuals, and the walk-through where I stood in for the president was notable for the honest enthusiasm the employees exhibited, swarming me in their rehearsals (the Secret Service emphasized that everyone would remain behind the ropes during the actual event, and they did, with polite energy).

But my major memory from the IBM visit is the prodding I had to take from Jim Kuhn.

Jim Kuhn was the president's personal aide, or "body man," as the press sometimes put it. Jim was affable, diligent, and the nearest thing to a member of the Reagan family. He greeted the president first in the morning, was the last to leave him at night, and traveled with the president on every trip. He would often call the advance team if something about the schedule wouldn't work for the president, or to check on a detail that wasn't clear. Jim always briefed the president in the motorcade and often whispered names of local officials to smooth introductions. He was a friend to us, and a godsend.

Now I waited outside the IBM main entrance with the senior executive from the facility, ready to receive the motorcade. My first time to direct an arrival. As the limo turned in, flags fluttering on the front fenders, I realized with mounting horror that I wasn't sure how to initiate the visit. Should I greet the president, or introduce him to the IBM VIP? I was standing there more or less frozen with my mouth open. The president emerged from the back at the same time Jim Kuhn popped out of the front seat. Taking me gently by the arm, Kuhn said, "Lead, Terry, just lead the way." As I collected my wits, the president chatted briefly with his host. After a perfectly natural photo op, they turned and followed me into the plant. That wasn't so hard. Kuhn just smiled. He had seen many rookies.

The rest of the visit was a fine success; the employees cheered wildly, but remained behind the ropes, the president oohed at images of computer chips under a microscope, and Hooley clapped me on the back and said, "Fine job." But I'll always remember that initial Jim Kuhn cattle prod with embarrassment.

\* \* \*

Waterbury was to be a major rally on the historic green in the center of town. Hooley had visited Waterbury several weeks before on a "pre-advance" with Mike Deaver. The reception from the local Republican establishment was decidedly lukewarm. Connecticut was solidly Democratic. The locals predicted a rally would flop. Deaver scheduled it anyway. Now, mere advancemen were to make it happen.

The first morning Hatfield reported on his late-night survey of the Waterbury bar scene upon his arrival. He rhapsodized about a particularly enchanting local, Genevieve: "She spoke French and I went wild." This became an office catchphrase we repeated sophomorically at our countdown meetings, as in "I met with the editor of the newspaper today. She spoke French and I went wild." Hatfield vowed a news blackout on his additional nightlife adventures.

As usual, we set up a courtesy meeting with the mayor, Edward Bergin. Because Bergin was a Democrat, our expectations were low, but, to our surprise, Bergin was enthusiastic about President Reagan's visit and offered to help in any way he could.

Part of the reason was revealed in the story he told about his father, mayor of Waterbury in the 1960s. In a golden memory of almost mythical proportions, Bergin recounted how John F. Kennedy had scheduled a rally in Waterbury early in his campaign for president. It was not yet clear how much appeal Kennedy would generate. On top of that, the Kennedy motorcade was delayed for several hours, and it was presumed the crowd had gone home. So the Kennedy party went directly to their hotel, which backed on the green. Hearing chanting, they went out on the balcony to find five thousand fans who had remained into the night to see their candidate. Kennedy spontaneously addressed them from his balcony like the pope in St. Peter's Square. The press swooned, the Kennedy magic was kindled, and the elder Bergin was forever associated with the political springboard to Kennedy's election.

Now Ed Bergin wanted to repeat his father's glory and wasn't going to let a pesky detail like party affiliation interfere. He was also a patriot who honored the Office of the President, and had a keen appreciation for the economic benefit a presidential visit could bring to Waterbury. So we left our meeting great pals of the mayor. On the next day, Hooley, Hatfield, and I were sworn in as Honorary Police Commissioners of Waterbury, Connecticut, dubious for Hooley and me, and surely the only favorable connection Hatfield had ever had with the police. My "proclamation" read:

> WHEREAS: The success of any public event is directly dependent upon the Dedication and tireless efforts of those directly charged with such Awesome responsibility; and
>
> WHEREAS: That dedication was ever apparent during Wednesday, September 19, 1984, for the visit of President Ronald Reagan to the City of Waterbury; and
>
> WHEREAS: The events surrounding that historic visit to our community relied Heavily on individuals who demonstrated the inherent abilities to coordinate, organize, and analyze those necessary factors to insure the safety of so many; and
>
> WHEREAS: Terry Baxter and his associates have given of themselves freely to our City to make September 19, 1984, an unforgettable moment in Waterbury history.

NOW, THEREFORE, I Edward D. Bergin, Mayor of the City of Waterbury, do hereby Bestow "HONORARY WATERBURY CITIZENSHIP" upon Terry Baxter, and appoint him "HONORARY POLICE COMMISSIONER" with all the rank and privileges therein.

The presentation came complete with a handsome gold Police Commissioner's shield. All of which greatly disgruntled our local official, Greg Batterson. An energetic Republican partisan, Batterson was forceful and gruff. He seemed to have an effective local organization, which he ruled with an iron fist. His main focus was the local congressional race. His candidate faced a strong headwind from the heavily Democratic district. Batterson's strategy had been to distance his candidate from President Reagan. His outrage that the White House advance team would consort with the Democratic mayor was more than he could bear.

The mayor was friendly and genuinely helpful. Batterson was prickly and controlling. His expressions were what the French would call a *tete a baffe,* a face that invites you to slap it. The choice of where to go for help was easy. We assigned Batterson to crowd raising and office management while we spent most of our time with Mayor Bergin to prepare the site with bleachers from the football stadium, formulate traffic control, recruit high school bands, erect speaker and press platforms, and complete the many details the mayor's contacts could smoothly facilitate.

After a short countdown meeting on the eve of the president's visit, Mayor Bergin hosted the three "Police

Commissioners" to a tour of all the Irish bars in Waterbury. He was popular and we were well-received. The supposedly Democratic locals were overwhelmingly respectful toward President Reagan, their fellow Irishman. They were proud he was coming to Waterbury and looked forward to welcoming him. I produced handfuls of tickets to my VIP viewing section. The evening included many toasts and bawdy Irish songs. It is entirely possible a generous amount of Guinness was consumed.

As the old-timer of the group, I eventually decided to call it a night. I left Hooley and Hatfield with the ageless mayor and went back to the hotel. In the lobby, I ran into Greg Batterson's deputy, Todd. Todd was a pleasant young college student volunteering for his first congressional campaign. He had a permanent beaten-down demeanor. Tonight he had apparently been posted for guard duty.

"Greg is waiting in the bar for you," Todd said ominously.

"Me?"

"Well, any of you who show up. He got to the countdown meeting and found you had all left with the mayor." Todd leaned closer and said, "He's been in the bar ever since."

"What does he want? Is there some issue with the event?"

"He is not happy."

I sighed. "Okay." Todd and I found Batterson brooding over a beer in the nearly empty lobby bar.

"Well," he said grandly, "the mayor's butt-boy returns."

Todd stood wringing his hands.

"Get us another round of drinks," Batterson snarled.

It was hard to be sure which of us was the most influenced by alcohol, but I judged it to be Batterson. I sat down. Three beers materialized.

Batterson quickly went from morose to querulous. "Why didn't you wait for me before starting the countdown?" he demanded, waving his arms.

"Greg, we had a room full of people. We didn't know where you were or when you might get there."

"Oh you knew how to call me, don't give me that crap." His voice was rising; his face was flushing. Sensing trouble, the bartender looked over at us. Batterson leaned forward. "You guys have been nothing but jerks from day one. When this event tanks, you'll never do another trip." Now Batterson was screaming. Spittle was flying from his lips. "We need you know-it-alls from Washington to keep the damned president the hell out of my state."

*The damned president* . . . I was outraged that a supposed member of our team could be so disrespectful. I felt a tremolo in my chest. My body heat rose. It was time to cool his jets. "You've had too many of these," I said as I reached over and poured his beer in his lap. Apparently, cold beer to the balls is not salutary. As the shock was still frozen on his face, I poured *my* beer in his lap for good measure. He grabbed my sleeve and ripped the arm of my suit coat out of the shoulder. My lizard brain reacted—last straw. Red mist suffused me. I uncorked a lovely roundhouse right that lifted Greg clear off his chair and deposited him several tables away.

Todd was laughing and clapping me on the back. The bartender said, "Nice punch." Amid the incongruous reactions,

I was horrified. I couldn't believe what I had done. I hadn't punched anybody since my school-yard days. I was immediately remorseful.

Batterson leaped up from the tangle of knocked-over chairs in a rage. The side of his cheek had split open, and he grabbed a white napkin to hold against his face. "I'm calling the police," he screamed. "You're finished." He started a frenzied dance around the room. "I'm calling Ed Rollins. I'm calling Roger Stone," he said naming campaign heavyweights I recognized. He charged out to find a telephone. I sat down in the lobby to await my arrest.

While Batterson agitatedly called the police from the front desk, then every number in Washington that he knew, I sat quietly, resigned to my fate. I deserved whatever happened.

It was at this critical moment that Mark Hatfield walked in. He looked at me sitting off to the side dejectedly, then at Greg Batterson holding the bloody napkin to his face while he raged on the telephone.

What happened to him?" Hatfield asked.

"I punched him."

"*What?*" His incredulous expression told me how bad it was.

"You guys are all toast," Batterson snarled from the front desk. "The police are on the way."

Hatfield went into full crisis mode. He pushed Batterson through the swinging doors into the hallway where he dressed him down. His speech went something like this: "Listen, you moron. I don't know what happened here, but the President of the United States is arriving here tomorrow morning. Do you want him to be greeted with a headline that says his staff had a fistfight in the hotel bar? *You* are the one who is making that happen."

It took five long minutes of Hatfield persuasion to make Batterson see that his career was also on the line. They returned from the hallway considerably calmer. Then the policeman arrived.

He was a stereotypically overweight patrolman who hitched up his belt as he pushed into the lobby with a swagger. He had been called out at the tail end of his shift; he was damned sure going to arrest someone.

Hatfield apologized for the officer's inconvenience. "It was just a spirited political discussion."

The policeman was not buying it. "I was told there was an assault."

"No, no, no," Hatfield said soothingly. "We've just been out with Mayor Bergin . . ."

The policeman's eyebrows shot up, his attitude ratcheted down several steps.

Hatfield continued in his reassuring way, " . . . and when we got back to the hotel there was a slight misunderstanding." I'm not sure if Hatfield flashed his Police Commissioner's badge, but it is not impossible.

The officer's shoulders slumped. His eyes bored into Greg Batterson, still holding the napkin to his cheek. "What happened to you?"

After a pregnant pause, Batterson said, "I fell down."

"Oh Jesus Christ," the policeman said disgustedly. He threw up his arms and left, talking to himself.

\* \* \*

Hooley called me the next morning at 6:00 a.m. "Get dressed and get down to the conference room." I always saved a fresh suit for D day, so I was rescued from having to pin my torn sleeve together.

Seated around the table were Hooley, Hatfield, and Batterson (still with his napkin). Also present was the Republican campaign chairman for the state. He was a Connecticut local, not surprisingly part of the hostile camp. A sour expression never left his face.

"Terry," Hooley said, "you are going to apologize to Greg, then the two of you are going to shake hands, then we are going to go do this event." I followed his instructions, relieved not to be instantly sent home, as I had expected.

As the drama seemed ready to approach denouement, the state chairman said, "I knew from the pre-advance that you guys would be assholes."

Jim Hooley looked astonished. "Terry wasn't even on the pre-advance."

"I wasn't talking about Terry."

I watched Hooley process the words as he struggled to decode the target of the insult. Deaver? Hooley himself? Hooley graciously let the remark pass, but I could see from his expression that the exchange had altered his perception of the situation.

Hooley and Hatfield headed to the landing zone where Marine One would bring the president. I went to the town green where the motorcade from the landing zone would arrive for the event. I was ready to lead, at least for the day.

The crowd was massive; "twenty-five thousand," the police said. The mayor would have his moment of history. The event was flawless, a colorful, happy, warmhearted reception for the president, on a beautiful Connecticut day. The football bleachers around the green were brimming. Large crowds laughing and cheering a candidate are the adrenalin of a campaign. Even jaded reporters can begin to feel it. It happened that day in Waterbury.

As the motorcade pulled away to return to the landing zone, I let out a relieved sigh. There was still an excited buzz among the departing crowd. The volunteers were high-fiving each other. Whole families were posing for photos on the presidential platform. Twenty minutes later, I was thanking my volunteers, distributing wampum, and exchanging addresses, when my radio crackled. It was Hooley.

"Baxter, how fast can you get to the landing zone? You need to get over here. The president is looking for you."

I looked around at the streets clogged with departing cars and pedestrians. "Jim, it would take at least thirty minutes."

After a pause, he came back, "Okay, never mind." He clicked off.

I was left to wonder what was behind the call. My imagination ran wild: the president publicly ripping off my epaulets and breaking my sword over his knee.

It wasn't until we all got back to the hotel that Hooley told me the president wanted to shake my hand in front of the whole staff to put a period on my incident. My heart fluttered with gratitude, but it was short lived. Jim next told me the team was breaking up. After a great opening segment of the campaign, we needed to spread our talents. I was to go to Corpus Christi, Texas, with Lanny Wiles as lead.

Disappointment filled me. I was in the doghouse after all. Hooley was dumping me. No longer on the A Team. I had no one to blame but myself.

\* \* \*

Jim Hooley became assistant to the president and director of White House advance in President Reagan's second term. Over the years since then, he has been the glue that holds the fraternity together. He is currently vice president, government relations for Clean Energy.

President Reagan easily carried Connecticut when the votes were counted in November. Candidate John Rowland won his election to Congress from Waterbury. He became Governor in 1995, serving three terms before going to prison for corruption.

Mark Hatfield has remained a close friend for more than thirty-five years. He is now the award-winning head of security for Miami International Airport. Congratulations, brother.

In spite of the gigantic chip he carried on his shoulder, I apologize to Greg Batterson for the scar on his cheek.

*To Terry Baxter*
*With appreciation and best wishes,*

**Official White House Photo.**

**Advancemen-to-be greet President Ford (note that the author once had hair on the top of his head instead of the bottom).**

**Caribbean castaways: Pat, Ashley (11 years old), Terry, Bryan (14 years old).**

**Mark Hatfield in one of his subdued moments.**

**Terry Baxter with Brent Johnston, Mark Hatfield,
and Jim Hooley between events.**

Official White House Photo.

**Lima, Ohio, turns out for Ronald Reagan
and the *Ferdinand Magellan*.**

The Lima team poses with a portion of the
Lepo Brothers' mural.

Courtesy of the Reagan Library.

**President Reagan signs the mural at the Lima train station.**

Baxter and Ambrose with Art Fleming under
the arch in St. Louis.

Embassy drivers Joel and Thierry, Terry Baxter,
and eau de vie cellar master.

Terry Baxter and James C. Miller III in the
White House Roosevelt Room.

Official White House Photo.

**President and Mrs. Bush arrive for their inaugural gala, greeted by Terry Baxter and Joe Canzeri.**

Gregg E. Mathieson.

**Baxter and Canzeri bond over the inaugural gala.**

Courtesy of the Reagan Library.

The "Presidents and the First Ladies" at the rehearsal for the Reagan Library dedication. Shelby Scarbrough is second from the left in the first row; Andrew Littlefair is second from the left in the back row.

Courtesy of the Reagan Library.

The gathering of presidents for the Reagan Library opening (Nixon had departed after Pat Nixon was overcome by heat).

Courtesy of the Reagan Library.

**While studying his script, the author inadvertently holds the president's arm...and gets THE LOOK.**

Courtesy of the Reagan Library.

**President Reagan's jaunty reaction to "catching" Baxter gripping his arm. Jim Kuhn is at left.**

**Jack Byrne with Pat and Terry Baxter.**

Dear Terry "One Punch" Baxter — My appreciation for all you've Done & Warm Regard.
Sincerely — Ronald Reagan

**Official White House Photo.**

**Baxter eventually earned credentials.**

# TEXAS TWO-STEP

## CORPUS CHRISTI, TEXAS

### SEPTEMBER 1984

I spent a few days in Washington before reporting to Texas. I got a call to come to the RNC (Republican National Headquarters) to sign a few papers.

When I gave my name to the receptionist, I was met by an attractive young lady and escorted upstairs. She led me into a room full of small cubicles and announced, "Ladies and gentlemen, this is Terry Baxter." The room broke into applause, a few standing. Several came over to shake my hand, somewhat nervously, I thought.

"What is all this?" I asked my unknown escort.

"These are our political coordinators. Many have been screamed at by Gregg Batterson."

I was uncomfortable, but comforted. "So, " I said trying to make sense of the summons, "no papers to sign?"

"No papers, just a little feedback."

I found myself smiling as I left town.

\* \* \*

If I hoped the grapevine would not reach all the way to Texas, my bubble was burst when I reported to the staff office in Corpus Christi to confront a large boxing poster pinned to the door. Lanny Wiles, the Corpus Christi lead, was a happy-go-lucky good old boy. "Come over here, son," he said, gesturing to the poster with an infectious smile. "Make a fist. I want my picture with you." While the fight aftermath was rapidly getting tiresome, I knew right away we would be friends.

But Lanny was also an inveterate practical joker. On my second day in Texas, I returned to the office to find a phone message from "Gregg Batterson's lawyer." My face fell. I barely noticed the hush in the room. With mounting dread, I tried to call the number as everyone in the office pretended not to watch. The number was fictitious, but I still worried that the message had been accidentally transposed. There were smiles all around at my credulity. Lanny finally confessed that he had made it up. "Sorry. Just a little advanceman humor."

Lanny was also a great storyteller. He rattled them off rapid fire. My favorite was the time he had been held hostage at gunpoint by a deranged belligerent named Charlie. President Reagan was playing golf in Georgia, I think it was. All his Secret Service agents were on the course. Lanny and presidential aide David Fischer were in the clubhouse when Charlie confronted them and demanded to talk to the president. In Lanny's telling, the lengthy standoff that resulted was only salvaged by his incredible courage and persuasive charm. I've since been told most of this is true.

We went out every night to a little Texas nightclub that featured the Texas two-step and country songs. "If you're going to play in Texas, you've got to have a fiddle in the band" was a staple. It became our place to blow off steam. Tom Pernice was my assistant on the site, a recent UCLA grad with wavy black hair and movie-star looks. He received the majority of attention from the local girls. Our two-step was laughable, but the warm atmosphere helped us enjoy the time off.

Our site was an airport rally for the president's departure. I deployed my usual tricks: sets of bleachers to rim the crowd area, backed by another set of bleachers mounted on flatbed trucks; high school bands; and an invitation to teachers, Cub Scout, and Brownie troops to bring their children to see the president, which added parents and brothers and sisters to the crowd. This time I had another asset: Lee Greenwood had agreed to come to sing his anthem, "God Bless the USA," in person.

How could Texas not be enthusiastic about a president whose Secret Service code name was Rawhide? And they were. As the large crowd swamped us, we scurried back and forth to get the school bands in the upper bleachers with the class groups in the front ones. I worried that we would fill the entire area between the border of bleachers and have no room left to accommodate latecomers, but arrivals finally slowed to a trickle just before the president's appearance.

I got the bands playing and sent Tom Pernice over to the school groups to rehearse some patriotic chants. As he choreographed their efforts, several of the teenaged girls shouted, "What's your name?"

"Tom."

Almost immediately, the entire section came back with their own ad lib: "Tom, Tom, he's our man. If he can't do it, nobody can." Tom covered his face and blushed, which only produced several more renditions of the chant.

I laughed and went to investigate just what chants Tom was rehearsing. He held his arms out in a gesture of innocence while the kids squealed with delight. The cute little blonde teacher stepped out of the bleachers with a student in tow. "I want to get my picture with the two of you," she said. So we posed while groups of students yelled catcalls. "Oh Tom, Tom. This way Tom." He smiled. More cameras flashed.

By the time the president arrived, the crowd was primed for a Texas hoedown. He didn't disappoint them. Their energy fed each other. Lanny Wiles beamed like a proud father.

At the conclusion of the president's speech, Lee Greenwood was supposed to launch into his song from a little side platform with a balloon rise to accompany it. But as he touched the keyboard of his electric piano to get ready, a loud hum came from the speakers. The huge, bear-like WHCA lead ran up scowling and said to Greenwood, "If you touch those keys again, I'll break your fingers." Greenwood looked thoroughly horrified.

I grabbed the WHCA agent by his arm and said, "Hey, leave my talent alone."

He towered over me. "He's screwing up the sound system."

"It's your job to make the sound system work, so make it work."

I noticed Dick Darman and several of the senior staff observing the exchange bemusedly, probably wondering if the red mist would engulf me. The president completed his remarks to thunderous applause. Greenwood looked at me uncertainly.

"Go ahead," I prodded. He played. He sang. The balloons rose. All was right with the world.

* * *

It was rare that we got to enjoy the glow from the president's visit with the locals. More often we would fly off immediately to the next stop. But that night we stayed over. When we arrived at our little two-step nightclub, we found a giant banner across the top reading, "White House Staff Here Tonight." The parking lot was packed. We gestured back and forth between our two cars. This might not be the best choice. We were debating the wisdom of going in when the proprietor emerged to escort us. A cheer erupted as we entered. Beers were thrust at us from all directions. The room was hot and crowded.

It was quite a party.

Texas girls surrounded Tom Pernice. The little blonde schoolteacher from the rally rushed up and grabbed me by the arm. "Every blonde in Texas must be here tonight," she blurted. "I thought I'd better get to you first." I smiled and let her guide me through a clumsy two-step.

She held onto my arm and leaned on me. Her lips parted. "Wherever you are going next, I want to come," she said.

I was honestly floored. We hadn't said two sentences to each other, but she wanted to abandon her job to join the campaign trail. It never occurred to me that campaigns could create such avid groupies.

I realized, of course, I was unnaturally blessed with manliness and sex appeal, but this was too much. She was not unappealing, but as Paul Newman used to say, when you have steak at home, you have no need to shop for hamburger. My discouraging frown told her everything she needed to know. She turned abruptly and made a beeline for another advanceman. After Texas, I would regularly remind myself that campaigns drive people crazy.

Perhaps this explains Joe Biden.

\* \* \*

Tom Pernice, still one of my favorite colleagues, became the director of advance for the vice president in the second term. He then returned to California to form his own public relations company.

Lanny Wiles, a lifelong friend, has remained a heavyweight political consultant for three decades. He most recently headed the advance operation for John McCain's presidential campaign.

# FERDINAND MAGELLAN

I finally felt like my rehabilitation was gaining momentum when I was given my first lead for the president's visit to Lima, Ohio.

The trip was a dream. The local party folks were so warm, we departed as old family friends. The Republican mayor, Harry Moyer, threw all of his resources behind us. Everyone was full of good ideas ready to work hard. My premiere helper, Carol Thompson, and her neighbors and colleagues, Allen County Republican chairman Bob Holmes and "Mr. get-things-done," Ed Kirk, are fond memories.

The stop was part of a Jim Hooley extravaganza involving Harry Truman's 1948 whistle-stop campaign train borrowed from the Gold Coast Railroad Museum in Miami, Florida. The *Ferdinand Magellan,* built in 1928, had also logged 50,000 miles as FDR's Presidential Railcar, U.S. Number One. The presidential car included a rear platform with loudspeakers mounted over it, where President Reagan addressed the people gathered trackside as the train traveled five miles per hour from Dayton to Toledo, Ohio. Several intermediate stops included Lima, where the train would pause for a major rally.

For the Reagan trip, the train was called *The Heartland Special*.

Our site was the old Amtrak train station in Lima. The space was bare and scrubby. Across the track was the dingy cinderblock wall of an old warehouse. The team already had plans to dress it up.

I always sent volunteers to locate the largest American flag they could find. Usually, car dealerships were a good bet. Lima's gang already had a huge flag nearly big enough to cover the cinderblock wall, which would serve as the backdrop once *The Heartland Special* pulled in. If only I had staff like this on every stop. No one blinked when I described the rest of what we needed: bands, bleachers, flatbeds, press platform, speaker's platform, tickets, press passes, flags, signs, and miles of rope and stanchion.

To fill the bleachers, we concocted a "battle of the bands" open to all the area high schools. In the end, six bands participated, rocking the pre-show. Then some genius introduced me to two local artists, Bob and Dave Lepo, who were willing to paint a mural on the cinderblock wall if we would buy the paint. They said they could feature the famous *Shay* locomotive, produced by the Lima Locomotive Works for more than seventy years. The photos of their previous work convinced me at once. Painting began that same day.

This freed our giant American flag for another mission.

We had a pair of charming young advancemen, Fred Corle and Mike Lake, who were assigned to visit all the farms along the train's route. The instructions were to give a general approximation of the train's slow speed passage time and invite the families to stand along the side of the tracks to greet the president. Corle and Lake spent day after day chatting with farm families.

In the meantime, the president was participating in the first debate with Walter Mondale. I watched the debate on television with the Lima host committee. Reagan seemed confused and tentative. Over the next several days, Reagan's age became the subject of a media debate. His staff contended he had been tired and over-rehearsed. Perhaps he was experiencing a transient episode of Alzheimer's, which would be officially diagnosed much later.

We knew he needed a lift more than ever. At the final countdown meeting, the Secret Service reported, "We might have a problem." The lead agent's face was grim. With hundreds of miles of track to defend, the agents had reason to be nervous. "There have been some activists meeting with farmers along the route. They may be planning some kind of protest or disruption. We haven't been able to pin it down. We have two names," he flipped through his notes, "Corle and Lake."

The advance team laughed in unison. "Not to worry," we said, "they are *our* guys."

After the countdown, I went over to a pep rally held by the host committee, now numbering in the hundreds. The mayor's speech about how Lima could restore the president's spirits brought pride and cheers from every participant. The mood was a perfect send-off for the grueling day that would follow.

The Lepo brothers' mural had turned into a masterpiece. The artists had transformed the cinderblock wall into the inside of an old-timey train station, with a beautifully rendered

Shay steam locomotive seen through the arches. Just in front of the locomotive stood a depiction of Ronald Reagan in a stationmaster's uniform, consulting his pocket watch.

A portrayal of the lead Secret Service agent, Mike Young, was pulling an old-fashioned baggage cart, and I was pictured in a bowler hat next to a pretty damsel in hoop skirts and a parasol. All it needed was a few little girls, which one of my volunteers proceeded to supply, complete with period dresses and parasols. We built a small platform to place them in front of the mural. While naturally nervous about anyone behind the president, the Secret Service eventually signed off.

The weather gods smiled on us. The crowd swelled to nearly the entire population of Lima, the bands battled vigorously in the massive row of bleachers, and *The Heartland Special* pulled in front of our mural with the little girls twirling their parasols and waving to the president. The president gestured to his colleagues inside the train car until all the senior staff had crowded on the platform to wave back.

As "God Bless the USA" was performed, our giant American flag rose up behind *The Heartland Special* by the magic of the Lima Fire Department's hydraulic rescue lift. At the conclusion of the song, an entire hopper car full of balloons was released, rolling up and around the fluttering flag into the clear-blue Ohio sky. Sheer poetry.


I had one more dash of color I hoped to add. I outlined my plan to Hooley and he said, "Go for it."

I had prepared some words for the emcee, just in case: "Mr. President, Lima has a proud history as a railroad town. By happy coincidence, rail road and Ronald Reagan have the same initials. We hope you will honor us by signing your initials on our mural."

The crowd started to roar. The president dipped his head in his modest and genial way and went over to the platform where the little girls were still wiggling. He crouched down and thanked each one at eye level. Then he took the brush and red paint I had planted and signed "R R" on the wall.

Hooley later told me the senior staff called Lima "the best stop of our best day ever."

One by one, *The Heartland Special* collected each of the leads from every stop. We gathered in the forward lounge. Meanwhile, the president stood on the rear platform and waved to little knots of farm families and well wishers all the way to Toledo. The pace was slow enough that Reagan could pick out individuals as we passed by. "Hello to the little girl in the blue dress. Thanks for coming."

Corle and Lake had done their jobs well. The entire route was lined with people.

As the train finally stopped in Toledo, a radiant President Reagan came into the lounge car to thanks us. When he saw me, he said, "Ah, one-punch Baxter, winner and still champion." My colleagues were still laughing and jostling me as the president shook our hands. As he greeted me, he made a fist, leaned in and whispered, "I think I could take you."

\* \* \*

For hours after the stop in Lima, people singly or in groups came up to pose in front of the mural, pointing at the president's initials. I was told the town sprayed the surface with acrylic to preserve it as a historic site. I hope that is true.

For thirty years the Lepo brothers, now well-known artists, have produced private, public, and corporate art with a concentration on sculpture.

One of the little girls got a spot of red paint on her dress from a drip as the president signed the wall. She showed it off to reporters and said, "I will never wash this dress again," an uncalculated and sincere moment the media loved (and a welcome contrast to Monica Lewinsky's blue dress years later).

In the second presidential debate one week later, Reagan was challenged by Mondale about his age. Reagan famously retorted, "I will not make age an issue in the campaign. I am not going to exploit, for political purposes, my opponent's youth and inexperience."

Even Mondale had to laugh. He later said, "That was really the end of my campaign that night."

# Days Counting Down

By this time in a campaign, the days rushed by, one day merging into the next. I only have a few clear memories, both trivial, from Amarillo, Texas, which I did with a capable new advanceman, Craig Patee.

First, I remember the night Craig and I accompanied the lead Secret Service agent to the Big Texan, a local steak house famous for their seventy-two-ounce steak. That's right, four-and-a-half pounds of beef.

While we waited to order, the agent told us stories from his years in law enforcement before the Secret Service. The one I remember was the time he arrested an extortionist who had kidnapped a bank president's wife in an attempt to force him to withdraw money. At trial, the defendant demanded to represent himself, and the demand was granted.

His big moment came as he questioned the wife on the stand. "Now Mrs. Jones, had I harmed you in any way before I put you in the trunk of the car?" He looked horrified as he realized he had just confessed to the crime.

"Objection," he shouted.

The judge could only shake his head. "I'm afraid you can't object to your own question. But I would entertain a change of plea."

The Big Texan had a standing bet that if you ate the shrimp cocktail, the potato, the roll, and the seventy-two-ounce steak in one hour, the dinner was free. Only two patrons had accomplished that feat in all of 1984. Our Secret Service lead was determined he would earn a free dinner. Craig and I ordered more modestly.

The entire production was quite a show. Our steaks arrived sizzling, accompanied by a parade of waiters announcing, "Ladies and gentlemen, we have a contestant. Try not to break his concentration." Then they started a large clock on our table.

At first our agent made rapid progress. The shrimp cocktail disappeared in less than a minute, as did the roll. Patrons crowded around us to take pictures. Hunks of potato and steak were consumed in obvious pleasure, but at two pounds, the chewing became arduous. Chants of encouragement swept the room at random moments, but the agent was struggling.

With ten minutes to go and tension mounting, more than a pound of steak and a quarter of potato remained. The agent chewed on. At two minutes to go, he shoved everything remaining on his plate into his mouth, now so stuffed he could barely move his teeth.

At the bell, the room applauded. The manager leaned in and said, "Don't choke yourself. Take your time to chew it all. You'll get it free."

The agent threw up his arms in victory, but he was clearly suffering. It was more than forty minutes later when he took his last swallow. It had not been fun. When I went on the website of the Big Texan to try to remember his name, there was no listing for October 1984.

The second thing I remember is that we had a senior staffer from Governor Bill Clements' office to manage our staff office. After three days of bonding, she wangled a certificate from the governor commissioning me as an "Admiral of the Texas Navy." I consider it a treasured keepsake.

* * *

Then it was on to Medford, Oregon, a rugged, beautiful portion of the state. A mere thirty miles north of California and situated in the mild Rogue Valley, Medford had beautiful weather in October.

I had a completely new team. Suzie Trees was the press advance, and Matt Crow was my site advance, another handsome young stud. Even with the compressed time schedule, we had a cohesive and happy group. Our local contact was Hugh Jennings, a Reagan delegate since 1968. Widely known and respected in the area, he was the Reagan–Bush chairman for Medford, and another goldmine of local knowledge and support.

Our event was an airport rally, so we started with the best possible backdrop: Air Force One, which would pull up directly behind the speaker's platform. While Matt Crow worked with Hugh to move the grandstands and build the platforms, I rehearsed two high school bands with help from the WHCA lead.

My plan was to replace the usual recording WHCA provided with the town's two high school bands playing "Ruffles and Flourishes" and "Hail to the Chief," the traditional introduction to the president. The student musicians were overjoyed at the prospect of being an official part of the president's visit. I owe kudos to WHCA for allowing this departure from the standard practice. Mere bureaucrats would have said, "No way."

With grudging approval from the airport, we mounted a hundred-foot pole with a cross piece at the top on the west side of the viewing area. We had a lumberjack champion who would climb the pole with nothing more than spikes and a leather strap, and then, at the conclusion of "God Bless the USA," unfurl the giant American flag. Crowd pleasers all.

The big disappointment came the day before the event. The head of the local Democratic Party threatened the high schools with a lawsuit charging that the schools were using city property—the band instruments, uniforms, and school buses— for a political event. He suggested the school administrators would probably lose their jobs.

One after the other, the school officials caved; they called me to withdraw their approval. There would be no high school bands. I was heartbroken for the kids. I called WHCA to prepare them for the recordings after all.

I went to bed quite depressed about human nature, but just after midnight, I got a call from a high-school parent. She told me that all the parents were outraged to have their children jilted after so much practice and excitement. Together they had resolved to bring the children themselves in a private caravan of cars, with practice instruments from home, and handmade uniforms. Her intensity brought a tear to my eye. I told her we would save places in the grandstand for the kids.

* * *

The Oregon sun shone on Ronald Reagan. Air Force One made a magnificent sight as it taxied into position. The students played the warm-up songs all dressed in matching T-shirts labeled, "NOT the Medford High School Band." Somehow they had produced them overnight.

The president waved from the door of the plane, then greeted some dignitaries behind the platform. The on-stage emcee called for silence, then one "not" high school band performed an excellent "Ruffles and Flourishes." The WHCA announcer intoned, "Ladies and gentlemen, the President of the United States." The president came on stage to a tumultuous welcome while the other "not" high school band played "Hail to the Chief." I smiled with tight emotions.

President Reagan spoke movingly, then stood open-mouthed while the lumberjack scampered up the pole and the American flag flew in the afternoon light. Hugh Jennings gave me a bear hug and said, "You sure have made it easier for me here in Medford."

I had the chief of police in his dress blues and two young Girl Scout champion cookie salesmen in uniform waiting behind the stage for a photo with the president. The photo was on the schedule. But on departure, Reagan just rushed right past me without looking. He waved goodbye to the rally throng from the door of Air Force One and disappeared inside.

I grabbed Jim Kuhn's arm as he passed. "Jim," I said urgently, "I had a photo op."

"Yeah, the last stop had *twenty-five* locals lined up for a photo op. It's out of control. No more photo ops."

"Jim, I have never abused a photo op. I only have two."

"Who?"

"The chief of police and two Girl Scouts who sold the most cookies."

"Oh god. Okay, wait here." Kuhn went up into the plane and quickly returned, gesturing. "Bring them into the plane."

My lucky guests were going to get a much more coveted remembrance: a photo with the president in his private quarters aboard Air Force One. The little girls posed on each side of him with their favorite box of Girl Scout cookies.

"Now, can I buy these?" Reagan inquired like he was requesting a great favor. They looked at each other like they might faint and nodded. The president patted his pockets. When he looked up at me, I got the message. He rarely carried cash. I quickly passed him two tens. "Here, this adds to your record," he said, handing each girl a ten-dollar bill.

The little girls climbed down the steps from Air Force One hand-in-hand with the chief of police waving the money. They were swarmed by a gaggle of Girl Scouts and parents from their troop.

A near miss.

* * *

An angry debate about the school bands raged for weeks in the local paper. It was generally considered a massive black eye for the Democrats. In the fall, a new local Democrat was named chairman. Hugh Jennings wrote a lovely letter to the president quoting John Chancellor's televised comments, "President Reagan's airport rally in Medford, Oregon, was the best orchestrated political rally I ever saw in my life." After several unnecessarily restrained comments about my contributions, Hugh Jennings wrote, "Terry and I remain friends to this day, and will always." Someone on the White House staff put an exclamation point next to this statement before passing the letter on to me.

I never got my twenty dollars back.

# MILLERSVILLE STATE COLLEGE

Fall was in the air when we got to Lancaster, Pennsylvania, and the campaign was in the final stretch. It was nearly Halloween.

I loved being back in the East. I grew up only thirty miles away in Harrisburg and many of my high school friends were still in the area. Even better, we were close enough to home that my family could drive up from Washington to see the event. As if my blessings weren't already overflowing, I got another new site advance, Chris Ambrose, the best of the campaign.

Chris Ambrose was big-boned and lanky. The hollows of his cheeks colored in the presence of a pretty girl. At twenty-two years old, he was six five, with hands large enough to palm a basketball. And handsome. What was it with this succession of young matinee idols? Could I ever be paired with a middle-aged bald guy? No, apparently only budding chick magnets: Jim Hooley, Mark Hatfield, Tom Pernice, Matt Crow, and now, Chris Ambrose. But Ambrose offset his looks with a happy-go-lucky charm and an absolute determination to get the job done. If I was the smoothie that Bob Tuttle claimed I was, Ambrose was the exuberant puppy dog that smothered you with happy licks until you succumbed.

Our rally would be in an indoor arena on the campus of Millersville State College. Millersville was established in 1855 as the Lancaster County Normal School (teacher's college). In the heart of Pennsylvania Dutch country, it boasted a beautiful campus of about twenty-five hundred students.

The arena already had a full set of stadium seats, so our biggest job was already accomplished. Chris built the speaker's platform and we decorated with hay bales and pumpkins for the season. We commissioned a large backdrop with the somewhat wordy slogan, "Pennsylvania Dutch Country, Dutch Reagan Country!"

The college administration was very supportive, but was concerned about the capacity of the arena. At three thousand seats, the room could barely accommodate the students and faculty, and of course I wanted thousands of seats for the general public. We finally agreed that I would get half of the tickets and the college would get half of the tickets, with areas for standees and press.

This led the college to announce it would offer the free tickets on a first-come-first-served basis on the morning before the president's visit at 9:00 a.m. At the same time, we were fending off ticket requests from Republican groups throughout the area. We felt like Broadway producers with a blockbuster hit on our hands.

With preparations almost complete and a full day ahead to tidy up, we all went out to a leisurely dinner at one of the excellent Pennsylvania Dutch specialty restaurants. When we returned to the campus, we found a long line snaking around the administration building where the tickets would be dispensed the next morning. Hundreds of students were planning to wait all night to secure a spot in the arena. We were touched and gratified.

"Get some trinkets," I said. We went down the line shaking hands and exhausting our supply of presidential memorabilia, but feeling exhilarated. The coeds all wanted to hug Ambrose; I had to constantly prod him to move along. Whenever I became discouraged by cynical press comments about the campaign, I remembered the kids sleeping outside all night just to experience it.

The next day, the local afternoon paper ran a photo of a middle-aged couple in a sleeping bag. The caption said they were waiting in line all night on behalf of their children who had to study for finals. With only two tickets, they wouldn't be able to attend themselves, but thought the experience of seeing a president in person was too important for their children to miss. The accompanying story interviewed four or five students who had been in line, but missed the cutoff. They were mostly philosophical. Some said they planned to cheer by the roadside as the motorcade arrived.

But I knew the president would arrive by helicopter on the far side of the arena. There would be no motorcade. I felt sorry for anyone who would be disappointed, but maybe I could help a few. I grabbed a volunteer and handed him the newspaper. "Get me the phone number of everyone named in this article."

He was a good detective. He got me the number of the sleeping-bag couple, as well as four out of five of the disappointed line-standers.

I called the couple first. I got the mother. She confirmed they were the subjects of the story. I introduced myself and told her, "I am arranging the president's visit to Millersville. Here is my phone number. You can tell your children to give their tickets to roommates or something. I would like to invite you and your family to be guests of the president in our VIP section right in front of the podium."

There was a pause as the words sunk in, then she started yelling, "Harold. Harold, come here right away!" I felt like John Beresford Tipton, distributing surprises on the old TV show *The Millionaire*. I told them what entrance to use, and suggested they ask for me when they arrived. I alerted all of the volunteers to be on the lookout for them.

I also reached all of the students from the newspaper who had missed the cut-off and offered each of them a spot in the VIP section. The joyous whoops and thank yous echoed in my ears. I actually did feel like a million bucks.

D day arrived with rain, making the landing area muddy. We hastily covered the marshy grass with large sheets of plywood to make a solid path into the arena. The sun came out just before the event. Reagan luck.

My wife, Pat, and two children arrived, along with Pat's brother and his wife and son. I had little time to talk, but was overjoyed to see them. I sat them in the VIP section along with the sleeping-bag family and some of their fellow students.

I can't remember a campaign moment that brought me more satisfaction.

"Signal arrive" sounded in my earpiece and I rushed for the landing zone.

\* \* \*

## GATEWAY ARCH
St Louis, Missouri

The last stop of the campaign before heading to California was St. Louis, Missouri. Chris Ambrose and I were still a team, which was great. Rick Ahearn, another pro on the full-time White House advance staff, also flew in to help. Rick is revered for being the cool-headed lead advanceman on the day Reagan was shot in an assassination attempt in 1981.

I arrived in St. Louis to find a picture of my ten-year-old daughter, Ashley, holding a homemade Reagan sign on the front page of *USA Today.* Apparently, the photographer in Millersville found her as irresistible as I did.

Our site was the park under the Gateway Arch, a massive national monument that rivaled anything in Washington, D.C. From the arch, the park sloped down a grass embankment to the Mississippi River, forming a natural amphitheater. Everything about the site was perfect for a large crowd except that heavy rains the previous week had swelled the river and threatened to overrun the access road and staging area for the platform and arrival tents. We crossed our fingers and erected the set and the press platform. Our backdrop proclaimed, "Gateway to

Victory," with a depiction of the arch, since it was up the hill and behind the cameras.

We nervously checked the flood reports every morning.

For planning elements, we also had everything we could ask for. Art Fleming, the original host of *Jeopardy*, had agreed to be our emcee. He was funny and irrepressible, and became a great friend. If Art's humor flagged, we had Bob Hope (yes, *that* Bob Hope) to introduce the president. We had the Purdue Marching Band and the Golden Girls, and we had a massive crowd coming to see the St. Louis Cardinals play for first place in the NFL East in nearby Busch Memorial Stadium.

The game was to begin an hour after the president's scheduled arrival, so we distributed fliers that said, "Come to see President Reagan at the Gateway Arch. Park early, before the rush. Enjoy refreshments and entertainment. Then walk to the football game in time for kick-off."

The day before the event, the river had crept to within feet of the access road. The positioning of our stage, only yards away, was just too perfect to abandon yet, but we were apprehensive. As a fallback position, we prepared a small riser with bunting, electric power, and microphone leads. It was safely on the top of the hill, high and dry. The press could use it as a panoramic cutaway position. If need be, we could redirect "stagecoach" (the president's limo) to the riser, even at the last minute.

Overnight, the river seemed to hold level. Maybe it had crested!

For such a large crowd to filter through the metal detectors, we broadcast the need to come early. It worked. Football fans and voters alike began to fill the amphitheater three hours before the president's appearance. Fortunately, we had planned for several hours of entertainment to occupy the early arrivals. Art Fleming was a master at whipping up his growing audience. Riverboats sailed by on the Mississippi, which had started to fall imperceptibly.

I left Chris in charge of Art and the site, and Rick Ahearn to schmooze the VIPs with Bob Hope in the arrival tent, and headed off to the airport for the arrival of Air Force One.

Just when it seemed we had dodged every bullet, a new crisis raised its ugly head. Up 'til now, the campaign had ignored Minnesota, partly out of respect for Mondale, the favorite son. But new polls revealed we were within a few hundred votes in Minnesota. The campaign staff decided they should "leave no stone unturned." As a result, they called me from Air Force One to say they would make a "quick stop" in Minnesota on the way to St. Louis. "We'll be a little late," they confessed.

With a sinking feeling I asked, "How late?"

"Not more than an hour."

An *hour.* That would run the arrival right up to kick-off time of the football game. I reminded them that probably half my crowd held tickets to the game, and thousands had already been there for more than three hours. This was not the kind of last impression we wanted to leave.

"Do your best," they said. Winston Churchill whispered in my ear, *No, succeed in doing what is necessary.*

I called Chris at the site and he got Rick Ahearn on the line also. I explained the situation. They both groaned. "Rick, see if Bob Hope could do a little routine to keep the crowd engaged."

He ran off to check. "Chris, give Art Fleming a bottle of Scotch and tell him to rehearse a human wave or something."

Rick called me back in a breathless moment. "Mr. Hope can't do it. He only has material for the introduction."

I was flabbergasted. "What? He's been in show business for fifty years and he can't do a couple of minutes off-the-cuff?"

"What can I tell you, he says he doesn't have any material."

I felt like my feet were in cement. "Okay," I said dejectedly, "we'll get there as fast as we can."

I was standing on the tarmac at Lambert Field, watching airplanes land that were not Air Force One, when an idea struck me. Over the three days we had been on the site, there were periods when the landing pattern brought aircraft right down the Mississippi River, past our site, to land at Lambert ten miles away. If Air Force One flew low past the site, the crowd would know the president was only minutes away. That might persuade some football fans to forgo the opening drive.

I called the airplane and presented my request. After several minutes of consultation the word came back: yes, they would fly down the river.

I exultantly called Chris to brief him. "Have Art watch for the plane. The airspace is closed to regular traffic, so if you see an airplane, it is Air Force One."

Back at the arch, the audience began to drift away. Chris Ambrose and Art Fleming anxiously scanned the sky. "There!" Chris yelled, pointing.

Art went to the microphone, his voice a fever pitch. "Ladies and gentlemen, I have just been told that by the direct order of the President of the United States, Air Force One is going to fly over to salute us for waiting so long." A loud cheer arose. Some of those departing actually paused.

"There it is," Art screamed. "Let the president hear us." The audience thundered in response and waved their arms at the sky. Art Fleming became positively giddy as he said, "Ladies and gentlemen, what a sight, the finest airplane that flies the skies, Air Force One!"

As the plane flew by, the lettering on the side became visible. "Pan Am," it said. It was the press plane, which usually precedes Air Force One by about a minute. But Art had created such hysteria; it is not clear how many noticed the discrepancy. Hopefully they thought the "second" appearance of Air Force One moments later was a victory lap.

* * *

*Time Magazine* used a photo of President Reagan from Millersville for the cover of their election special edition. The photo showed the president, the hay bales, the pumpkins, and a portion of the backdrop. They cropped the photo so the slogan read: "Reagan Country!" *Time* also used photos of the president signing the Lima mural and a massive crowd shot from Waterbury, a trifecta.

Art Fleming sent me a Christmas card every year until he died.

# Election Night

In a blink, the campaign was over. It must be how the end of sudden-death overtime feels; a maximum effort for four and a half quarters, then, without warning the scoreboard shows a win. Great, but the balloon is still inflated.

All the leads from around the country were brought to the Century Plaza to share the final act. After four months of twenty-hour days and seven-day weeks, most of us slept through the first day.

Election night was staged in the Grand Ballroom of the Century Plaza, packed like a mini convention. Spirits were high and only grew as the early returns were announced. The advancemen were still working: managing the crowd as it pushed relentlessly closer to the stage; escorting the press pool to the president's holding room for photo ops, as he watched the returns; and cuing the music and preliminary speakers as the schedule played out. We were workers, but also participants, equally exhilarated when the size of the victory became evident.

In the end, Ronald Reagan won every state except Minnesota—which he lost by just 3,800 votes—and the

District of Columbia. He won 525 electoral votes, the most in history. I have to admit I felt sorry for Walter Mondale. He was smarter and a more honest and decent man than any of the higher-scoring losing Democrats who would follow: Dukakis, Gore, or Kerry.

We were called backstage by radio; the president was about to come out. We needed to form an aisle through the swarm of "special friends" between the holding room and the platform. Each excited, some bleary, all cooperated politely as we packed them to each side. "Pretend you are in a wedding photo," I said as I had to turn the Hollywood stars and socialites' shoulders sideways to fit them all in. They laughed good-naturedly.

President Reagan strode through the gauntlet like the conquering hero he was, hand-in-hand with Nancy, pausing to shake hands and whisper quips. The family paraded behind to join him on stage.

Reagan's acceptance speech brought tears and wild applause. Few of us were immune. Then I felt a squeeze on my arm. I turned to find Lee Greenwood. He smiled and held up his hands. No broken fingers. Then he dashed on stage to sing "God Bless the USA" one last time.

The presidential after-party was in a large suite upstairs in the hotel. The advance team had a suite down the hall. Besides celebration, we had a secret mission—when one of the guests in the president's suite showed signs of being over-served, the social secretary would tell them, "We would like to have you meet the people who made it all happen." A military aide would guide them to our suite where we were supposed to entertain them and ply them with coffee. Chuck Connors, "the Rifleman," and Charlton Heston, among half a dozen others, enjoyed our tender ministrations.

\* \* \*

## WASHINGTON, D.C.
November 1984

After flying back to Washington, I wandered through the campaign office. It was empty and abandoned. Headquarters had never been my turf. I had spent all my time on the road, but it was nevertheless depressing to see the silent cubicles and scattered papers. There was no sign that it had been the heart of a winning effort.

The campaign staff and the advance teams had dispersed. Now the president's appearances would be official trips and state visits handled by the White House Advance Office. I was told to expect a call from time to time, when the demands of a foreign trip made additional manpower necessary.

What a joy to be home with my dear ones. I was also excited to return to work at GEICO, although it had a touch of "down on the farm after seeing Paris." Some of my colleagues disagreed with my politics, or considered my absence a special privilege due to favoritism. I could understand the reaction. I would gain nothing by disputing it, but I didn't notice any of them foregoing four years of vacations. For the most part, my co-workers welcomed me back warmly and were excited to hear all the details of my adventure.

I had only settled in for about two weeks when, incredibly, I got a call from the Advance Office. "Would I be able to help orchestrate the inauguration?" I actually laughed outright.

"I've been away from work on and off for five months. I've more than used up all of my goodwill. Sorry, I have to focus on my job."

"But we want to assign you to the big television gala. Deaver wants you to be chairman. You are the only one who can do it."

I knew better to fall for that line. "Sorry, I really can't."

I thought that would be the end of it, but I confess the words lingered in my ears, "television gala . . . chairman." The next day when I saw Jack Byrne in the hallway, I ventured a query, "What would you think if I told you they have asked me to do the inauguration? We could actually involve some GEICO people."

Jack dismissed the question with a wave of his hand and said, "I would say enough is enough."

I nodded. "That's what I told them." I felt guilty that I had even mentioned it. Jack walked away, shaking his head. I *really had* used up my goodwill.

A few days later, Jack walked into my office and sat down heavily. He stared at me like I was supposed to confess something. "What?" I said.

"I just got off the phone with the chief of staff to the president of the United States," Jack said, continuing to watch me closely. I realized he thought I had put Mike Deaver up to calling.

"What? What? Are they naming you ambassador to Ireland?"

"No. Mr. Deaver thanked me for all of our many sacrifices, seconding you to the campaign and all, then he told me about this television gala that virtually pays for the whole inauguration, and how you are the only one who can do it, and how for the good of the entire nation and little puppy dogs, I had the rare opportunity to . . ."

He had me laughing now. "Jack, I already told them I can't do it."

"Well, I told him you *could do it.* I think I even told him it would be our honor."

"No, really . . ."

Jack held out his hands in a "stop" motion. "Look, Terry, what do you say to the second most powerful man on the planet? I said yes. Go make us proud . . . prouder."

So began another great adventure. But now I was back in Washington, the land of political intrigue, a land that was populated by people who got where they were by whom they knew rather than what they had accomplished. I had left the heartland where colleagues smiled in front of you *and* in back of you. When someone wants to help you in Washington, there is always a hidden agenda.

So, I shouldn't have been surprised when I met with Mike Deaver and Ron Walker at the inaugural headquarters and they told me I was now going to be *vice* chairman of the gala. "Mrs. Reagan has one of her little darlings, Joe Canzeri. She wants him to be chairman, so there's not much we can do. But, *you* will be the real boss. You will have the budget authority. If Joe gets in your way, just wave the checkbook at him."

I had never heard the name Joe Canzeri. I had no preconceived notion, but obviously Ron Walker did not like him. Mike and Ron stood, and motioned me to the conference room. Margaret Tutwiler, a kind and attractive veteran of the State Department, was waiting. She was the director of public liaison for the inaugural. We knew each other slightly, but both accepted Deaver's introduction to each other as if it was necessary.

"We've got Canzeri waiting in the anteroom, cooling his heels," Ron Walker said with obvious delight. "He thinks he is a thousand-pound gorilla, but he is only a hundred-pound gorilla. We're going to bring him in here and let him know we've got him by the balls."

Margaret Tutwiler seemed to perk up at the prospect.

Joe Canzeri walked into the room . . . with Frank Sinatra.

*What an entrance.*

Deaver and Walker were mute.

Canzeri was hardly the imposing figure I had imagined. He was short, maybe five four, and stocky. He had that northern Italian tanned complexion and affected a white scarf hanging around his neck to accent it. But he commanded the room, even in the company of Frank Sinatra. Charming, and exuding easy confidence, Canzeri launched into a twenty-minute monologue about how "he and Frank" saw the talent line-up for the gala evolving. No one had a question.

At the end, Sinatra told a funny anecdote about the time he went backstage to meet Luciano Pavarotti after an opera triumph. Sinatra asked Pavarotti, "Maestro, how do you close off those high notes without the tone ever wavering?"

"Is easy," Pavarotti replied, "you shutta yo mouth."

We all chuckled. Sinatra and Canzeri got up to leave. Deaver at last emerged from his coma. "Joe, Joe," he said by the door, "I'd like to have you meet Terry Baxter. He did all our best stops of the campaign. I'm sure he will be a great resource to you."

Joe looked me up and down and shook my hand. He never said a word.

After they left, I turned to Deaver and Walker and parroted, "I'm sure he will be a great resource . . . We sure got him by the balls." The two midgets looked sheepish. Margaret Tutwiler laughed.

\* \* \*

The gala had a small group of offices at inaugural headquarters, but Canzeri had decamped to the Washington Convention Center, the event site. He already had an embryonic staff transplanted from his public affairs firm, The Canzeri Company. I heard he told them, "Deaver has appointed a spy [me] that no one should talk to."

I decided there was no choice but to confront our situation head on. I called him and said, "Joe, we don't know each other. Let's have dinner and try to figure out how to make this work."

"Sure," he said with little enthusiasm. He named an Italian restaurant in Georgetown. By now, I had gathered some background on Joe Canzeri. He was generally considered a good guy. I hoped he was hearing the same about me.

Canzeri had been conscripted into politics while managing the White Face Inn in Lake Placid, New York. The New York governor, Nelson Rockefeller, admired the way Joe served as "Mr. Fixit" over a visit to Lake Placid. Joe had an uncanny talent to anticipate every need and effortlessly execute each detail. He took pride in accomplishing the impossible. Rockefeller invited Joe to join his campaign staff, and later to manage the 1,700-acre Rockefeller estate in Pocantico Hills, New York. When Rockefeller was appointed vice president after Spiro Agnew's resignation, Joe came to Washington as senior staff.

After Reagan was elected, Joe Canzeri moved to the White House where he became a favorite of Nancy Reagan. He left under a cloud in 1982, after an ethics probe brought unwelcome attention to the administration. He was exonerated after a lengthy investigation.

Canzeri had a reputation as "an advanceman's advanceman." The underground word had him once badgering the Park Service into lighting Mount Rushmore in the middle of the night so Rockefeller could see it as they flew over. He was obviously my kind of guy.

Our dinner began awkwardly. I thought of it as a peace conference; Joe was determined to keep his distance. He was not hostile, just inaccessible. Gradually, after a couple of glasses of wine, our mutual experiences made conversation easier. We told war stories. The exchanges warmed. When we finally got to the business of our meeting, I simply said, "Joe, I'm not into office politics. I am not in anyone's pocket. I have no mission here except to do the best damned inaugural gala of all time."

He listened, but he was noncommittal. I left feeling I had accomplished nothing. Not for the first time, I asked myself if I was crazy to jeopardize my job and to miss Thanksgiving, Christmas, and New Year's to join this team that didn't want me. I contemplated calling Mike Deaver to bow out.

Out of the blue, Joe Canzeri called me the next day. "If you want to help the gala, get the contract signed."

"What contract?"

"The contract for our producer, Mike Seligman. He does the Academy Awards, for chrissakes, without half the trouble the Inaugural Committee is giving him. I've been trying for two weeks to shake his contract out of the counsel's office. We're on the verge of losing Mike."

I can't say my experience with lawyers had always been positive. In my opinion they often said no because it was the safer course, the coward's way out. Lawyers at work were always telling us what we couldn't do, not how to properly do what was needed. So I was not optimistic as I sought out the counsel's office at inaugural headquarters.

I count it as an incredible stroke of luck that Chuck Sabo was the guy with the stack of papers on his desk, which included Mike Seligman's contract. He seemed inordinately happy in his windowless office. He welcomed me like he had never entertained a visitor before. When I mentioned the Seligman contract, he actually found it in less than thirty seconds.

"I've been trying to figure out who this guy is," he said. He held the contract like he was weighing it. "He has a pretty heavy set of conditions."

"Chuck," I said, "he is the real deal. We need him. He is the producer of the Academy Awards. He's got five weeks to pull together a five-million-dollar television gala for the president, and we are jerking him around."

"No one told me it was important." He started flipping through the terms. "What do you need?"

"Your sign-off."

"Really? Okay." He reached for a pen and signed it.

My jaw dropped. My best ever interaction with a lawyer. Canzeri was stunned when I dropped it on his desk an hour later. I think I felt the earth tilt on its axis. Joe went to the next door and told his colleague from the Canzeri Company, "Sorry, you'll need to move your stuff. Terry is going to be here now."

Joe liked decisiveness and so did I. He would carefully listen to a request. When he was satisfied about the essential details, he waved his hand and said, "Basta," which must mean "enough" or "done" in Italian, because it meant he approved; he had given his word, which he always honored. So I guess the contract episode was our Basta moment. The acrimony was forgotten; we were now a team.

Michael Seligman was on his way to Washington from California that very afternoon.

We met the next day with Frank Sinatra, the *honorary chairman* of the inaugural gala (chairmen were proliferating daily). We started a list of potential talent for the show with Canzeri's secretary making notes. Sinatra would personally call to recruit them once we had approval.

When we gathered to review the typed list, we came across the name "Barry Shinkoff." It took several minutes of head scratching and trying to remember our recommendations before we realized the secretary had not recognized our suggestion of Mikhail *Baryshnikov*. We all had a good laugh. We also found ourselves dodging unsolicited talent offers from major donors or GOP honchos. It was surprising how many had a favorite niece who was a "wonderful singer."

After a week of give and take, and the usual issues of availability, we had assembled a terrific list of performers: Sinatra, Dean Martin, The Beach Boys, The Gatlin Brothers, Lou Rawls, Don Rickles, Donna Summer, Ray Charles, Mac Davis, Rich Little, and Mikhail Baryshnikov. We also corralled celebrity hosts for introductions and historical footnotes: Pearl Bailey, Patricia Neal, Jimmy Stewart, Merv Griffin, Tony Randall, Elizabeth Taylor, Robert Wagner, and Tom Selleck.

Then, the inaugural brain trust decided we should do a second gala, the night before, honoring the vice president, so we cobbled together some extra artists, Frank Sinatra, Jr. and Kathie Lee Johnson, to join Rickles, Martin, Rawls, Little, and the Gatlins, who all agreed to do two performances.

Mike Deaver had ordained that the president and Mrs. Reagan would sit in the arena seats like any other patrons, but Nancy Reagan overruled this idea. She wanted a platform with throne-like seating. This meant we had to disassemble several rows of the elaborately telescoping arena seats to construct a platform. The only way the manufacturer would warrant the conversion was to send a team of factory mechanics from

Europe to oversee the job. We had to entertain them for several weeks so they could reinstall the seats after the gala.

For every morning we ground out insurance contracts, music licensing, union agreements, or catering arrangements, we enjoyed an afternoon of major talent rehearsals from just off stage. Joe and I rarely left each other's side.

We were lucky to have a cadre of guardian angels like Chuck Sabo. One of them was Mr. Joseph, a top aide to the mayor of Washington, D.C. A distinguished, silver-haired black man, Mr. Joseph was built like a football linebacker. He described his specialty as "shredding red tape."

In his introduction to me, he said, "If you have a problem with anyone in the D.C. government, they will be having a problem with me." He told me his fee was "one front-row ticket."

It was a price I was happy to pay. In fact I told him with a smile, "Bring a friend, if you have one." His assistance would turn out to be invaluable.

The convention center seating charts were in constant flux. The telescoping arena seat sections were fixed, but as with the president's platform, other seats were removed for camera placement and the vice president's platform. Seats were reserved for the press and the Secret Service, and seats behind television camera positions would have a blocked view, so I advised not selling them.

On the floor of the convention center, nearly four thousand seats would surround the stage on all sides. The committee dithered about creating "boxes" of ten seats each, which could be priced higher, and if so, how many? Every day we set up tentative arrangements for the committee to preview, while the fire marshal scurried around with his tape measure to check the width of the aisles. Finally we all agreed on a plan. The fire marshal, still grumbling and pacing with his tape measure, signed off. We had settled on dozens of boxes, and for each one, the original tickets had to be pulled and replaced with newly printed tickets for "Box One," etc. Box One, for instance, now sat where seats in row A, one through five, and row B, one through five, had previously resided. Each box eliminated ten numbered tickets. A detailed list of the tickets that needed to be removed from the vault was sent to Colonel Klink in ticket sales. (Yes, *that* Klink.) Numerous follow-up phone calls confirmed he understood.

In the final week, events flashed by in a blur. Tense excitement built by the day. The salute to the vice president on Friday night gave everyone a chance to stress test our final plans.

Friday night was not televised, so the start time could be a little flexible. Dwight Hemion, the television director for the gala, used the performance to preview his lighting and camera shots for the live show on Saturday night. Getting the audience through the magnetometers, properly seated by the ushers, and returning their coats and hats promptly all proceeded smoothly. The military bands in the entry hall and the pre-show of the US Naval Academy Glee Club Choir maintained a steady drumbeat of entertainment from the time the patrons entered the main entrance until they departed. Vice president and Mrs. Bush were gracious in the limelight and the show was lively and well-received. It felt like a successful out-of-town opening.

We fell into an exhausted yet contented sleep Friday night.

D DAY
January 19, 1985

We had the final dress rehearsal for the 50th Presidential Inaugural Gala just after lunch. We had decided to open the rehearsal to White House staff and more than twelve hundred came. This required ticket-printing and distribution, and security screening, but it was well worth the trouble. The performers loved playing to an enthusiastic audience rather than an empty room, and our White House colleagues appreciated the thoughtfulness.

The site was cleared at three o'clock and the Secret Service sweep began. My team of volunteers arrived, mostly personal friends and executives from GEICO, all dressed in tuxes. They would be my eyes and ears and crisis-response team. I left to put on my tuxedo.

By the time I returned, the "green" room was an exciting bustle. The talent enjoyed each other as well as a fabulous buffet Joe Canzeri produced with Rockefeller's former chef.

For the patrons, we had "The Taste of America" in the entry hall, a sample of chefs' creations from across the country, to entice gala-goers to come early. It worked like a charm. The performance hall was filling rapidly. Jack Byrne and his family arrived to claim one of the boxes, and a number of other GEICO executives were scattered throughout the hall. I was gratified to have them participate in such a momentous event.

Then, with twenty minutes to show time, the Colonel Klink crisis exploded.

Secretary of State Shultz arrived with his party to discover his front row box already occupied. The people occupying the box were *Mike Deaver's guests.* How could things get worse?

When I arrived on the scene after a frantic radio call, I examined the tickets and realized immediately that Klink had sold row A and B tickets that should have been shredded. A quick check of the adjacent boxes revealed more of the same. Three boxes, thirty tickets!

"Mr. Secretary," I said to a patient George Shultz, "I'm going to give you the best seats in the house." I turned to the best of my tuxedoed team captains, Ron Hamway, and said, "Get me thirty chairs in thirty seconds."

Ron ran into the hallway where a military band was playing and yelled, "Stop playing. Put down your instruments. Follow me."

Like good soldiers, the band members ran with Ron to the storeroom. With the bandleader angrily waving his arms at the rear, Ron and the band rushed toward the stage with armloads of chairs. We set them up in groups of ten immediately around the stage.

I saw the crimson-faced fire marshal charging toward us with his tape measure. I turned to find Mr. Joseph in his front-row seat and beckoned him.

Mr. Joseph analyzed the situation in a millisecond. The fire marshal said, "You can't . . ."

Mr. Joseph interrupted him. "What direction is that?" he asked, pointing to where we were hastily creating three boxes.

"Direction?" the fire marshal stuttered. "East."

"Good. Face west," Mr. Joseph directed. After a minute or two, the fire marshal got the message and stalked out of the hall. Mr. Joseph returned to his seat with a wry grin, but I still had another angry customer. The band director grabbed me by the arm. "What do you think you are doing? These men are musicians, what is the meaning of this?"

"I'm sorry," I said, "I promise never to do it again."

Just then the secretary of state came over and shook the bandleader's hand. "Thank your boys for helping out," he said. He gave me a nod.

The bandleader's lips moved, but nothing emerged. Color returned to his face. He finally said, "Do you think anyone got a photo of that handshake?"

Nothing can top the presence of the President of the United States. When Ronald and Nancy Reagan entered the convention center that night to the usual pomp and circumstance, the crowd met them with the pent-up emotion of a long and historic campaign. Even the performers, accustomed to responsive audiences, soaked in the extra energy. Nelson Riddle and his orchestra, Frank Sinatra and his talent recruits, and the military bands and glee clubs outdid themselves.

But my favorite act was the least-known, Michael Davis, an inventive and uproarious juggler. He began by announcing soberly, "I intend to juggle this everyday egg." Then reaching down into a gym bag, he said, "Along with the natural enemy of the egg, a bowling ball." He proceeded to juggle half a dozen raw eggs together with the bowling ball. Hilarious to see. At one point, while he juggled tennis balls and bowling pins, he spontaneously tossed one of the tennis balls to George Shultz, who was now nearly sitting on the stage. Shultz deftly caught it and threw it back, whereupon Davis incorporated it back into his rhythm without missing a beat. It brought the house down.

At the end of the evening, Ray Charles performed "America the Beautiful." As he began the second stanza, all of the entertainers returned to the stage to sing together with the audience. As the song concluded, the president and Mrs. Reagan stepped on stage. He was supposed to invite the vice president and Mrs. Bush, who were positioned at the end of their aisle, to join them, but Reagan forgot. He started thanking the audience for their support. . . .

Henkel was screaming in my earpiece, "He forgot the VP, he forgot the VP."

I crawled in my tux from my seat to the front of the stage. From the floor below the president I began to make frantic "V" and "P" letters with my fingers. Reagan looked at me quizzically, then I saw his eyes shift to the aisle where George and Barbara Bush had begun to march toward the stage on their own. Reagan laughed at himself and slid effortlessly into a gracious introduction of the Bushes.

Even with some small glitches, probably unnoticed by the viewers, we were all elated with the show. The gala team headed to the post-party with high spirits and broad smiles.

Pat and I stayed at the convention center to thank all the volunteers and to ensure the coat check and departures went smoothly, so we were about an hour late for Frank Sinatra's after-gala gala at the Shoreham Hotel. It was a mob scene outside the ballroom entrance. Apparently a large group of party crashers had been removed only moments before.

As we attempted to enter, an agitated woman rushed over and demanded, "Why are you here?"

"We're here for the Sinatra Party."

"Who invited you?"

"Mr. Sinatra."

"Well, I am *Mrs.* Sinatra, and I don't know you from Adam."

Fortunately Joe Canzeri saw us at the door and saved the day. "Mrs. Sinatra, I'd like you to meet Pat and Terry Baxter. Terry was vice chairman of tonight's event."

"Oh, I am so sorry, it's just been so awful. . . . Please have a good time."

And we did—one more glorious evening mingling with the glitterati before returning to real life.

\* \* \*

Mike Seligman was instrumental in kick-starting my second book, *The Ursa Ultimatum*. Mike wanted to try producing dramas and movies, not just entertainment specials, so he nagged me to write an outline for another suspense thriller. He took it back to Hollywood to shop it around. While Mike made the rounds out West, I sent the outline to my agent, and the publisher agreed to buy it on the basis of the outline. *The Ursa Ultimatum,* dedicated to Mike Seligman, came out in 1988. It is another not-to-be-missed read from the Amazon out-of-print-bookshop.

I am still waiting for Mike to call me with the movie deal.

Joe and Tricia Canzeri remained dear friends for the next twenty years. We vacationed at each other's homes, or shared Nantucket rentals, or sailed and partied together. Joe died in 2004. I will always feel the loss.

We produced somewhat garish white leather jackets for the cast and crew, with the gold seal of the 50th American Presidential Inaugural Gala embroidered on the back, and their names in gold script on the front. I made sure there was a jacket for Chuck Sabo, Ron Hamway, and Mr. Joseph.

Dartmouth College experimental scientists recently tested students with a functional magnetic resonance imaging procedure—fMRI—to see what brain reactions were generated by viewing a variety of social images. When the graduate students suspected they were getting false positives, they retested the MRI by substituting a frozen salmon purchased at the local supermarket. Sure enough, the dead fish tested positive for brain activity when "shown" the same social images. I wonder what they would have detected if they had tested Colonel Klink.

# JUDD SWIFT'S REVENGE

Judd Swift was a well-liked advanceman known for his practical jokes. He was portly and caustic. He somehow seemed to be moving in all directions at once and spoke like a buzz saw with a lisp.

Judd worked with Andrew Littlefair for a number of years. They were Mutt and Jeff: Littlefair, tall, courtly, well-dressed and good looking; Swift, short and rumpled. Littlefair was one of the fulltime Advance Office pros. Swift was a more or less permanent site guy. But all agreed he was a good advanceman and fun to work with.

One of the things holding Judd Swift back was his fear of flying. He really hated it, but obviously, flying was one of the essentials of the job. So, early in the 1984 campaign, Andrew Littlefair decided to retaliate for all the Judd Swift practical jokes with a little flight training.

Andrew assigned Swift to an event in the Midwest. Not just anywhere in the Midwest, but in a town carefully selected for the number of flights large and small required: Washington to a

Midwest HUB; Midwest HUB to a major town; major town to eventburg by puddle jumper.

Oh, one other thing, *there was no event.*

Littlefair told Judd to hit the road at once. The tickets were all prepaid. Swift would find a fax at his hotel with additional details once he arrived. As soon as Judd set off with a nervous look, Littlefair told everyone about the scam-in-progress. After nearly a full day of flying and changing planes, Judd arrived at his hotel and found an envelope just as he expected. But the message was a bombshell, "Judd Swift, you have just been HAD by Andrew Littlefair."

Judd called the office. We crowded around the speakerphone. "Littlefair, you bastard," he said. "What about the event?"

"No event," Littlefair said.

"No event?" Swift moaned incredulously, "Never any event? You are a rat bastard. I bet you expect me back tonight?"

"No, I've paid for your room tonight. Get a nice steak and come back tomorrow."

"How thoughtful. Don't think a steak is going to make me forget this, Andrew. Oh God, so tomorrow I have three more flights?" We all made airplane noises in the background.

He hung up.

Judd Swift let five months pass while he plotted his revenge. He considered several schemes, but it was his close friend in the California governor's office who brought full flower to his imagination.

Littlefair was a California native who intended to return to the state after the election to begin his career in politics. How to use his ego to entrap him?

With the help of his California friend, Swift printed an elaborately engraved invitation, complete with an authentic embossed California State seal, announcing that Andrew Littlefair had been selected as "Young Californian of the Year." The accompanying letter on official stationery invited Andrew to be honored at a black-tie dinner at the state house in Sacramento and to deliver an acceptance speech.

To say that Andrew totally fell for this is a massive understatement. He proudly toured the inaugural headquarters, showing off his invitation. He ordered a tux. He made his flight reservations. And he wrote and rewrote his remarks.

For the last weeks of the inaugural preparations, he read various portions of his acceptance speech to each of us to test reactions. It took every ounce of our self-control not to give away the game, but we had made a pact and kept it.

A few days after the inauguration, Andrew Littlefair flew off to California, still making corrections to his remarks on the plane. On the big night, he parked at the Capitol building and tried several entrances. They were locked. The building seemed deserted. He checked the invitation. Yes, he had the right date.

He still suspected nothing.

He walked the steps to the main entrance, and to his relief, the door opened. There was a flash as a photographer took his picture as he entered. *Thank goodness, I've found the right spot.*

The photographer stepped forward and said, "Andrew Littlefair?"

"Yes," Littlefair replied with a practiced smile.

The photographer handed him a letter. With suspicion belatedly rushing to his brain, Andrew had torn the letter open. Another flash went off. The letter said, "Andrew Littlefair, you have just been HAD by Judd Swift."

Sweet, cold revenge.

\* \* \*

Judd Swift created a beautifully framed display. It included the invitation, the photos of Andrew expectantly entering the Capitol, and the moment of horrible recognition as he read the letter. Sheer artistry.

Andrew Littlefair, who probably deserved to be the "Young Californian of the Year," but wasn't, began a long and successful California business career. He is currently the CEO of Clean Energy.

# Tales from the Road

Good stories like Judd Swift's revenge make the rounds of advance teams. Some are best told without too many specifics, including names. So the following tales will use proxy names. I cannot confirm or deny that any included my participation.

The team was advancing the Moscow summit. Before departure, they had a State Department briefing where they were warned to expect listening devices in their hotel rooms. "Don't embarrass yourselves, or us, by talking about the Russians," they were cautioned. "They'll probably hear everything you say."

The team was riding back to the Moscow hotel after a fruitless day of negotiating with their Russian hosts. Every suggestion, if it came from the Americans, was treated with deep suspicion, and rejected. Even efforts to make arrangements more beneficial to their hosts were greeted with hostility. The advancemen threw up their hands, *the not-invented-here syndrome.*

So the lead decided to test the listening-device theory. "Listen guys, we'll all go to my room to talk about our meeting with the Russians. But remember, they may be listening, so we'll feed them some propaganda."

They gathered in the lead's room and spent several minutes talking about their Russian hosts in glowing terms. They stifled smirks. Then they reviewed the many items they had offered to favor the Russians, expressing disbelief their counterparts couldn't seem to appreciate how it would help them. "Maybe we aren't expressing our suggestions clearly. These guys are just making it harder on themselves," the lead concluded. Then he held his finger up to his lips and bid them goodnight.

The next day, their Russian hosts were immediately friendlier. They offered coffee and small Russian pastries. They had rearranged a portion of the schedule in line with the American's proposals. "We have been talking," they said. "Perhaps we were too hasty to reject some of your ideas."

The Americans had to force themselves not to share knowing looks.

Preparations for the visit progressed more cooperatively, and after a successful day, the Russians invited the Americans to dinner. Russian dinners apparently require iced vodka bottles and multiple toasts. Vodka is poured to the brim in shot glasses, no ice, just very cold vodka. Attempting to sip one's vodka brought immediate guffaws of derision; it must be the Russian way, one glassful, bottoms-up per toast.

Which was how it happened that our team staggered back to their hotel and gathered in the lead's room, holding each other up. The lead pulled their heads close together and whispered, "Let's find the bugs." Faces immediately brightened.

Vodka-fueled laughter followed. The lead impatiently gestured with his fingers to his lips, until one by one they each followed suit, fingers on their lips and silly smiles on their faces.

They began to reel around the room, searching behind pictures, in lamps, behind the headboard. They became more hysterical as they searched, but managed to restrain most outbursts. When the lead pulled back the throw rug, he gestured excitedly. They all gathered, fingers on lips, but breathing hard.

A round metal plate about six inches in diameter was mounted in the wooden floor. Four large screws with thick slots appeared to secure it. *They had found the bug.*

Someone produced a quarter, which fit the slot perfectly. One by one they removed the screws. The last screw was harder to turn, and, as it came out, there was a loud crash in the room below.

They froze in horror. Then, as if in slow motion, they glanced up at their own ceiling, noticing the chandelier for the first time. *Oh my God.* The lead threw the rug back in place, and everyone scattered.

The next day, the Russians, not at all bleary, seemed solicitous of their new friends. "We hope you weren't disturbed last night. Apparently there was some excitement in the hotel."

"Oh?"

"A lighting fixture tore right out of the ceiling in a room near yours."

"How terrible. Was anyone hurt?"

"No. Fortunately the room was not occupied. Otherwise, we would have the trouble of looking for an explanation."

Vodka toasts, along with bug searches, were suspended.

\* \* \*

You have already heard that campaigns run on adrenaline. That is only partially true; campaigns also run on testosterone. Advancemen are the centurions of a campaign, the fighter jocks. Young and confident men, on the road for months at a time, advance teams become a laboratory of raging hormones surrounded by eager and attractive members of the opposite sex. This is as true for advancemen and women as it is for Secret Service, military, press, or traveling salesmen, and it always has been. That is not to deny that prudence and discretion should apply, but it is a fact of human nature that common sense sometimes takes a holiday.

One particular dashing young advanceman had three days to arrange a RON stop for the president at an oceanfront resort hotel. When checking into the hotel, he locked eyes with the appealing dark-haired receptionist. Over the next day, they exchanged smiles, bantered and flirted, and in the afternoon, he asked her to take a walk on the beach. She accepted.

By the day before the president's arrival, the signals were strong. He invited her to his room for a drink. She hesitated; her job didn't permit her to socialize with guests. She had already stretched the envelope.

Our advanceman pointed out that he had one of the private cottages down on the beach, away from the main part of the hotel. She would be able to visit without anyone noticing. The lead for the trip was a safe distance away in the main dining room entertaining the manager of the hotel for dinner.

Attraction was stronger than common sense.

The pair had drinks in the cottage, with a lovely private view of the ocean as the light faded. They talked, they kissed, and as the moon rose over the gentle ocean waves, they gradually surrendered to romance and passion. She was naked on the sofa, on all fours. He was poised to initiate intimacy.

Suddenly there was a flash of light. *Someone had taken a photograph through the picture window.*

The receptionist pulled herself into a fetal ball, "No, no, no . . ." she moaned in despair. *Discovered.* Her worst nightmare was coming true.

Our centurion leaped to the window in time to see the door to the main building of the hotel swing shut thirty yards away. He sprinted in pursuit, angry enough to ignore his nakedness. He pulled open the outer door just as a nearby room door slammed shut. He tiptoed down the empty hall. Was it the second door, or the third door? He listened at the second door, then moved on to the third. He heard children's laughter just inside. He banged on the door.

A boy of ten or twelve opened the door, wide-eyed at the naked apparition before him. The advanceman grabbed his shirt and said, "Give me the film."

"What film?" the little boy said nervously.

The advanceman's certainty was starting to waver when a girl's voice from deeper in the room said, "Give it to him, Joey."

The boy's resistance collapsed. He brought the camera from behind his back. The advanceman pulled out the film and passed the camera back. "You kids are little shits," he said, and stalked off.

Back in the cottage, the receptionist had started to dress. When her hero returned to display the film, she collapsed against him in tears. Soothing words, tender caresses, and calm persuasion gradually restored the romance. Clothes came off again.

Then came the banging on the door. The girl's emotions rose to hysteria again. The advanceman donned the hotel robe and went to the door. The receptionist pulled the sheet off the bed and wrapped it around herself.

At the door were the lead advanceman, the hotel manager, a policeman, and an unidentified man, his face twisted in anger. They pushed their way into the room. The manager's eyes grew wide when he saw his receptionist wrapped in a sheet. She buried her head.

"Is this your room?" the angry man demanded.

"Yes," the advanceman said.

"Then *this* is the guy," the man announced triumphantly.

Fortunately for everyone, the lead was Jim Hooley, a man well equipped to handle a crisis like this. "Okay, okay, let's just remain calm," Hooley said. "Everybody sit down. Let's find out what happened here." The receptionist remained buried in the sheets.

It was immediately apparent that the angry man was the young photographer's father. He started right in. "This guy," he said pointing at the advanceman, "came to my hotel room and accosted my children. He was naked."

"Holy shit," the policeman said, eyeing the advanceman. He looked like he had more questions, but Hooley pressed on, a regular Lt. Columbo.

The advanceman tried to speak. Hooley motioned him to remain silent. "How did he accost them?" Hooley asked.

"He grabbed my son by the throat and swore at him. He was obviously after my twelve-year-old daughter."

The advanceman jumped up and again tried to protest. Hooley again silenced him.

"How do you know this is the man?"

"My children told me which room was his."

"How did they know that?"

"I don't know. I guess they watched him when he went back outside."

"Okay," Hooley said, turning to the advanceman. "Your turn. What happened?"

The advanceman slumped in his chair. He knew the tale would be ugly. "Monique and I were having a drink in the room . . ."

"A little more than that, it appears," said the manager.

"Yes, okay, a little more than that. Some kids were outside the cottage peeking at us." His voice suddenly rose, "Peeping Toms—I guess we know how they identified my room—and took a picture through the window."

Mr. Dad's eyebrows shot up.

"I saw them run into the hotel and I chased them. When your son came to the door, I grabbed him by the shirt and told him I wanted the film. He gave it to me."

"So, you have the film?" the policeman asked.

The advanceman pointed to a canister sitting on the dresser.

Mr. Dad shifted uneasily in his chair. He was beginning to realize his little darlings might not be the innocents they had claimed to be. "You didn't grab his neck?"

"Only his shirt."

"Sometimes Joey exaggerates," Mr. Dad said with a shrug of contrition.

"There's still the indecent exposure," the policeman offered.

"How about invasion of privacy?" the advanceman shot back.

Hooley gave the advanceman a stern look. "Maybe you *each* would like to apologize."

The advanceman and Mr. Dad looked at each other for a beat, then said simultaneously, "Sorry."

"I guess I can live with that," the policeman said, starting for the door, "unless I get any more complaints about your guy running around naked."

"Thank you, officer," Hooley said. Everyone stood.

"Monique, get some clothes on before the officer notices that you are naked," said the manager.

The joys of parenthood.

\* \* \*

Of course, in life, as well as a campaign, there were also women who would exploit testosterone for their own reasons.

One was a strikingly beautiful lady we all met at the Reagan advance seminar in 1983. She was not a bombshell in the over-the-top body mode. Rather, she was a classy, sorority-girl type, with penetrating blue eyes capable of taking over your brain with a single laser gaze. She was magnetic in the way some movie stars or politicians can make you forget there are other people in the room.

While the full-time White House office girls were trying to impress us with their status—"Can you *believe* we get paid for doing this?"—blue eyes circled the room sizing up the prospects and fixing them with her high beams. They flocked to her like lemmings.

Ah, to be young again. After the campaign, where she had participated in a variety of stops, blue eyes attended the Reagan White House Christmas party on the arm of a prominent advanceman. She had moved up in the social standings, but not enough. She used the holiday White House event to train her blue laser on a variety of senior politicos. Her date became so exasperated with her behavior that he escorted her to the Northwest gate, and sent her home in a taxi, before returning to the party solo.

It wasn't long until she married one of the better catches from the Christmas party, a man of considerable influence, after which followed a series of increasingly visible administration appointments for his wife. It was a bonus that she was good at what she did, and she was soon playing on a national stage.

Her eventual divorce from her White House mentor led to another leap into rarified air in the international business community, and another marriage to the CEO of her company. She seems to be enjoying a happy marriage and a bourgeoning career.

A not uncommon Washington tale. While trysts, seductions, romance, and passion were not exactly rare, I never saw or heard of any member of the advance teams, including the Secret Service and military advance teams, patronizing a prostitute. Apparently times have changed.

\* \* \*

Jim Hooley was not only the driving force of the advance operation during the Reagan years, but he remains the focal point for keeping the gang together all these years later. He hosts regular cigar nights and pub crawls to keep the stories flowing and the friendships fresh. Recently, Jim told me a story I hadn't heard.

One of Jim's best full-time advancemen I will refer to as "Rhett" had a dilemma. Rhett had a new girlfriend, "Scarlett." Rhett also had a long-term friend, "Angelina," who was truly a soul mate, but not a romantic interest. Alas, Angelina was beautiful, smart, and funny—all compelling reasons for Scarlett to resent Angelina's friendship with Rhett. The immediate complication was that months before, Rhett had promised to accompany Angelina to a New York society wedding . . . you can't be unescorted to a society wedding . . . and the wedding was the next weekend.

Ever perceptive, Rhett's intuition warned him that Scarlett would not understand an away weekend with Angelina, no matter how innocent. "You've gotta send me on a secret mission," Rhett begged Hooley. "Cover for me. Nobody can know where I am."

Jim shook his head. "I know you, Rhett. You can't live with guilt; you will confess the whole thing in a week or two, then *I* will be in the doghouse with Scarlett forever."

"No. No. I can hold the line. It will be our blood secret. I will *never* tell."

Following more impassioned blandishments, Hooley eventually agreed. "Okay. Tell her what you have to, and if she calls me, I will say you can't be reached. Blood secret."

Rhett slipped out of town, leaving a note for Scarlett: "Back Monday. CONFIDENTIAL assignment." (Rhett was a man of many words.)

Hooley was entertaining house guests for the weekend. He got the first call on his red (White House) telephone early Saturday. It was Scarlett. "Jim, I *must* reach Rhett immediately."

"Sorry," Jim replied, "he is in an undisclosed location."

"But *you* can reach him, I know you can."

"Scarlett, it's confidential."

She insisted; he resisted.

The telephone calls intensified in the afternoon. Jim's guests were impressed by how often the White House needed to confer with him. Scarlett had escalated the drama to a "major family crisis." She said, "We are talking about life and death here." Jim was pretty sure whose death would be involved if he breached the secret. . . . He offered to try to pass on the details to Rhett, but Scarlett insisted that only she could talk to Rhett.

With increasing difficulty, Jim Hooley maintained his promised silence all throughout the next day, but he was exhausted.

Finally, Rhett called Monday morning. "Boy, those Russians can really drink vodka."

Hooley caught the hint. "She's right there, I suppose."

"Yes, I think I'm going to have a headache for a week. How's your end?"

"She was merciless, but I never gave you up."

"Great. I'll be a little late, but I'm coming in to brief you."

When Rhett got to the White House, they immediately retreated to Jim's office to coordinate their stories. Rhett explained that enterprising Scarlett had checked his closet to determine what clothes he had taken on his "secret mission." Her suspicions mounted when she noticed that his tux was missing and confronted him when he returned. Rhett said, "Frankly my dear, I don't give a damn." No, he didn't say that, he smoothly ad-libbed a "high-level Russian confab at an embassy black-tie function," and proclaimed exhaustion from the vodka and the intricate negotiations.

Jim rolled his eyes.

"Yeah, I know. It was the best I could come up with. She's skeptical. She'll keep digging."

Unknown to Rhett and Jim, quiet discussions had been underway for several months between the White House and the Kremlin to lay the groundwork for a major powers meeting. Days later it was announced that Reagan and Gorbachev would meet in Reykjavik, Iceland, for a historic arms-control summit.

Scarlett was still sulking when she heard the news. An arms control summit! She could hardly believe it; she had been so unfair. *Rhett must have arranged the entire conference.* He was a national hero! She greeted Rhett with a bear hug that night. "Oh Rhett. How could I have doubted you? You might be responsible for saving the world."

Rhett nodded modestly.

The October 1986 Reykjavik meeting broke the ice between the two leaders and led to a treaty eliminating intermediate-range nuclear forces, the first arms control pact to require reductions in nuclear arsenals.

The long and happy marriage between Rhett and Scarlett for the past twenty-seven years is another happy consequence of Reykjavik.

# European Parliament

With the turn of the calendar to 1985, I got two weeks of vacation time credited for the first time in four years. Pat and I actually started talking about taking a trip with the children. Vacation, what a concept.

While I was now a vice president at GEICO, a truly wonderful company, my heart remained with the Reagan team. I wanted to do more, I wanted to remain a member of the club. I expected to hear from Mike Deaver, or someone, about opportunities in the administration, but I learned Deaver was sick, and taking time off. Eventually I got a call from the RNC to come in for a job opportunity briefing for campaign veterans.

I found a roomful of Republican telephone bank operators, door-to-door canvassers, and a few lower-level county coordinators. Megan, a sweet girl I knew vaguely from some campaign stop somewhere, told us she was there to help us find an appropriate position in the administration. She appeared to be about twelve.

Megan circulated a questionnaire for us to fill out:

"What had I done in the campaign?" *Advanceman.*

"What had I done in the inauguration?" *General Manager, Inaugural Gala.*

"What position was I seeking in the Reagan Administration? I pondered the answer and decided this process was a waste of time. *Secretary of state*, I wrote, and passed my form forward.

Megan removed her glasses after glancing at my form. "Terry, we can't promise anything like this." She seemed so earnest and apologetic I almost laughed, but instead shrugged my shoulders and accepted my fate.

I was told later that Mike Deaver had gone into rehab for alcohol abuse. I didn't see him for the many months when he might have made a difference to my career trajectory. Deaver resigned from the White House in May 1985. But, I still had friends. Jim Hooley called to recruit me for the president's trip to Europe in the spring. Of course, it was a volunteer assignment, but Hooley said several irresistible words to me: "France, Walt McCay, and Chris Ambrose."

I talked it over with Pat; it was also her week of vacation time I would be using up to go to Strasbourg, France, for the president's address to the European Parliament. She knew I wanted to go and, as always, she put me first.

Strasbourg was special right from the very beginning. I was issued a diplomatic passport for the trip, which neatly snipped most of the red tape. The only sour note on arrival was that Ambrose had been shifted to Bitburg, where President Reagan's planned visit to a military cemetery had turned into a media circus. On the plus side, Janet Anderson, my old colleague from the Dole campaign, was the press advance, and Ed Russell, my favorite Secret Service agent, was the Secret Service lead. We had a new site guy, John Fisher, a cheerful young Californian from the family that owned a major clothing chain. He had the same gangling eagerness that made Ambrose so appealing. Our WHCA lead, Hasdovick, was on his last trip before retirement.

Alsace was a gloriously beautiful area of France near the German border. Heidelberg and the Black Forest are just across the Rhine. Alsace was annexed by Germany after the Franco-Prussian War in 1871. The area was returned to France by the Treaty of Versailles after World War I. Germany occupied the region again in WWII, then it returned to France after 1945. The shifting border and cultures have created a unique cuisine and architecture.

Strasbourg had become the center of European government. President Reagan's visit would include an arrival ceremony with full military honors, a short tour of the cathedral, a luncheon at the chateau, and the president's address to the Parliament of Europe. John Fisher would advance the chateau; I would do the Parliament; Walt would do the arrival, the cathedral, and motorcades.

After flying all night, I was a bit of a zombie, but Walt McCay had arranged a meeting at my site, officially called the *Palais de l'Europe*, at 2:30, so we all went for a walk-through. We met with the prefect (governor) who delivered several lengthy welcoming speeches—which had to be translated, ad nauseam, into English—while an entire room full of French police, military, and politicians waited to hear our reply translated into French; a forever way to have a meeting.

The next morning began with a security briefing. Bob Homme, the US counsel general for the region, had been shot four times in an assassination attempt only months before. He gave us a lecture on terrorists and how careful we should be. The office floors were guarded by marines, but not the sleeping floors. So much for peaceful dreams.

Later in the day, a little Piper Cub circled the hotel several times. We speculated it might be a "suicide Piper." When Walt went to the window, we yelled at him to "get away from the window, you make such a tempting target." He wrapped himself in the window drape and continued to peek until the plane left. Gallows humor.

We all went to meet the colonel who commands the French airbase where Air Force One was scheduled to land. Walt and I each had a car and driver. The cars were armored Chevrolet Caprices, with two-inch-thick windows. My driver was Joel, a delightful young Frenchman whose mother was on the clerical staff at the embassy. He spoke only a small amount of English, but did so with a flurry of gestures and great enthusiasm. The base headquarters was an undistinguished concrete building with a foul smell, but we'd only be on the airstrip. Pray for a sunny day.

Back at the Parliament, we went round and round about entrance, exits, and holding rooms for the president, the president's personal staff, the secretary of state, the official party, the pool, the US press, the foreign press, the invited guests, and Mrs. Reagan. It was amusing how the embassy people constantly pushed for the secretary to accompany the president on every move. The Secret Service and State

Department security were often at odds, and the motorcades were becoming truly elephantine.

My Secret Service site agent for Parliament was Barbara Riggs, a stout, no-nonsense law enforcement officer with a great sense of humor and first-rate organizational skills. The first thing she said to me was, "I intend to stay close to the president, so if he goes, I'll go too—no way I'm going up to Capitol Hill to testify . . ."

Walt, Janet, and I went out to dinner at the two-star Crocodile restaurant. Spring in Alsace meant fresh foie gras and fresh asparagus. The foie gras was new to me, but Walt and Janet were so eager, I ordered it in spite of the expense. I thought it was good, but couldn't quite understand what all the excitement was about. The sweetbreads, however, were spectacular.

No one had thought to brief Janet on the possible appearance of Big Boy, so she nearly fainted when he made a cameo visit. Fortunately, on this occasion, he was restrained in comparison to historical standards. Walt was so disarming, Janet was laughing in a minute.

I had left Joel in the bar so he wouldn't have to wait by himself in the car. Now, with cheerful innocence, he was too drunk to drive, so I would have to do it. We were lucky, no Jackals.

The next morning, it was off to the cathedral for a walk-through. Bob Homme conducted the tour. While we were scouting the avenue where the motorcade would have to stage, I noticed two suspicious men with bulges eyeing us. When we moved, they moved. My adrenaline surged. I touched my agent's elbow and cut my eyes over to the two strangers. "Bob Homme's bodyguards," the agent said with a wink. "Glad you are paying attention," he added to assuage my embarrassment.

A short walk brought us to another great restaurant, the Kammerzell, which produced asparagus with three sauces, and a salad with duck breast and foie gras. We ate all the way until our three-o'clock meeting for the arrival ceremony with the commander of the forces. Much translating back and forth seemed to achieve accord.

We finished the day with our first countdown meeting, about two hours, but at least no translating. The day before, John Fisher had picked up a lovely model at the cathedral and spent the evening pursuing her (hence missing the fabulous Crocodile dinner). When it was time at the countdown for John to outline the staff moves at the chateau, Walt said, "John will now discuss his 'night moves.'" A round of guffaws followed. Just at that moment, Chris Ambrose and Fred Corle arrived from Bitburg to spend the weekend with us (announcing their team was just too dull).

We all went out to dinner (Kammerzell again!) with Bob Homme. Over asparagus, foie gras, and Wiener schnitzel, Homme told us more about the attack on him. The first bullet shattered his glasses, went through his cheek, and exited below his ear. He was also struck on the neck and the arm. There was so much blood on his head, the terrorist thought he was dead, but fired a coup de grace into the heart to be sure. Since Bob was lying twisted on the seat with his suit bunched up, the bullet passed through the coat dead center of the breast pocket, but only grazed Bob because of the way his suit was twisted.

He was completely recovered and we all applauded his good fortune, but were sobered. We were forced to lighten the mood with several bottles of champagne and Alsatian Pinot Noir, which led to spirited renditions of ancient rock tunes and ringing our wine glasses by running our fingers around the rim until every French family in the restaurant was trying it.

After a fond farewell to Ambrose and Corle, it was back to work Monday morning.

We met with Secretary General Oreja of the Council of Europe, and the mayor of Strasbourg. French protocol made it absolutely impossible for anyone to make a decision, and therefore meetings were quite a disaster. The fun part was seeking agreement from the mayor, the prefect, the French police, the Council of Europe, the European Parliament, the State Department, the VO (the French secret service, *Voyage Officiale,* which is short for a longer name), the Secret Service, the military commander, and the White House. Somehow we were inching toward consensus.

Fortunately, the good places to eat dinner seemed to be inexhaustible. The two-star *Bueraisel* was the best yet, and the best dinner group: Frank McKay, head of the First Lady's detail, had just arrived; we also had Janet Anderson, Barbara Riggs, Ed Russell, Walt, and me. (John Fisher was still pursuing his model.)

Frank McKay was hilarious, regaling us all night with the massive preparations he had to make for the First Lady . . . so much to do . . . so many cars . . . never saw such a thick schedule . . . (Of course, as he knew, all miniscule compared to the president's considerations.)

The next day was another parade of negotiations ironing out more meet/greet/accompany/sit/speak/shake details. The State Department advance team was paranoid about the secretary of state getting second-class treatment, so trailed us everywhere like shadows. We called them our doppelgängers.

In a touching invitation, my funny French driver, Joel, invited us to his modest home to meet his parents and to try his father's distilled-in-the-barn *eau de vie,* or "water of life." *Eau de vie* was the local brandy distilled from fermented fruits, typically pears, cherries, and plums. Even John came with us, and Thierry, Walt's driver. But Joel was the star of the evening, obviously proud to have his American charges visit his home. His mother and father spoke no English. They watched the conversation swirl around them with befuddled smiles and chuckled when we all laughed.

After Joel had played the piano, his mother served some little cakes, then we all trooped to the barn for some *eau de vie.* His father lined up four tall shot glasses for each of us, with a sample of his various batches. He ignored our finger-measures asking for "just a little" and poured four full glasses of the clear liquid for each of us. He said something in exuberant French, which Joel translated, "You must leave my establishment feeling like Alsatians!" And we did.

The next day, May first, was a national holiday in France, so nearly everything was closed. We gratefully slept in. We had a brief morning countdown, which was mostly smooth except for the doppelgänger's complaints. Frank McKay missed the meeting (forgot), but said it was because he was arranging little model cars to "align" his motorcade (he has three cars) and was "analyzing" the First Lady's schedule (it's two pages).

That night was our long-anticipated trip to the famous three-star *Auberge d'Ill*, a truly outstanding dining experience. Joel told me I had "eaten more stars" in one week than he had his entire life.

I spent the next day in the doghouse. I created a diplomatic flap when I told the embassy I was using my guest tickets to invite Joel and his parents for the president's speech. I was sternly advised there was "protocol to consider." Many more important French would be insulted to see "ordinary people" in the gallery . . . makes you wonder what happened to the French Revolution.

I reiterated. They were my tickets, I would invite who the hell I wanted, protocol be damned. I was promised an earful from the fearsome Mrs. Masmejean, the French chief of protocol, when she arrived. They all seemed terrified to even say her name.

At the mid-day countdown, SY (State Security) made another macho speech . . . "We'll be coming through corridor X, and if anyone's in the way, we'll form a flying wedge to shove our way through." The Secret Service rolled their eyes. For the next few days, if Ed Russell questioned one of our moves, we replied in unison, "We will form a flying wedge."

I took Janet Anderson to have dinner at the *Maison de Tanniers* so we could check out the venue of Mrs. Reagan's lunch. They treated us like venerated pashas—we each had the local specialty *choucroute garnie*, a brimming plate of sauerkraut covered with a variety of sausages and ham hocks. Delightful. The high point was the teapot at the end of the dinner, a long droopy spout with an ornate head, which caused the ever proper and dignified Janet Anderson to say, "umm, looks like Big Boy." I nearly fell off my chair. She had come a long way in a week.

Sunday was a long day of walk-throughs. Jim Hooley came on the jump plane from Madrid to run through each site. I also rehearsed all my group escorts for the Parliament and met with the elevator operators. Naturally they all had an inflated view of their role, planning to hold the elevator door for the president, etc., until I emphasized that they would remain in the elevators at *all times*.

The French criers were also becoming a running comedy routine. It seems that every location had a crier (announcer) who must formally proclaim the president's arrival, or great loss of face follows. At the end-of-the-day countdown, I said as a joke, "As the president approaches the dais, the Parliamentary Crier, The Council of Europe Crier, the Strasbourg Crier, the Alsatian Crier, and the Boy's Club Crier will each announce him." The countdown meeting collapsed in hysterics.

We returned to the Crocodile for another great dinner: Walt and me, Jim Hooley, John Fisher, and Ed Russell. Jim Hooley was a fabulous mimic—he'd make a great actor and had wonderful tales. One of his favorite subjects was an advanceman named Gubatosi, who tangled the pronunciation even in his native language. Imagine how he butchered unfamiliar phrases. Overseas, he added Ms to every foreign word. The whole American and Chinese teams were under the table after one or two minutes of "Nakisomi coming to the Riki Rami Palace in Misam."

Jim related the time when wound-tight military aide Pete Metzger called the White House and got a language-mangling Gubatosi.

G: (falsetto voice) "Hello there."

M: Who is this?!"

G: "Well, golly, who is this?"

M: "I demand to know who this is immediately."

G: "I asked you first."

M: sputtering

G: "So, let me get this straight. You don't know who this is?"

M: "Precisely."

G: hangs up.

Next, Hooley imitated the interpreter during the pre-advance to China. As the Chinese VIP delivered his welcome toast, at each pause, the interpreter would translate, always starting with "Now he said . . ." at the top of his lungs. So the toast went something like this: "NOW HE SAID, we most joyously welcome you to our country."

Chinese.

"NOW HE SAID, we hope you will sincerely enjoy your stay."

Chinese.

"NOW HE SAID, we will strive to extend boundless hospitality," etc. The American team was desperately trying to suppress smiles.

Then Mike Deaver got up to respond. After his first sentence, the interpreter screamed out some Chinese, which they all knew must be "Now he said . . ." The team could constrain themselves no longer. They squirmed and smirked while trying to remain silent. Deaver was left with a long solemn toast while trying to maintain a straight face.

One more day of endless walk-throughs, compromises, seating changes, and disputes. The French had gone back on every promise they'd made; every agreement we thought we had was reopened. The French obviously feel that an agreement is merely concessions on our side while any of their concessions will merely be reinstated at the next meeting. I would hate to be a diplomat and have to deal with such dishonesty. The most troubling villain was Mr. Sedes, the Parliament's protocol officer. He seemed remarkably able to disregard every understanding we ever reached.

In the middle of all this, the fearsome Mrs. Masmejean, chief of French protocol, arrived. She turned out to be a delightful mix of Julia Child and Margaret Thatcher. We buttered her up by taking her to the *Buerheisel* for lunch. I was becoming quite fond of foie gras by now. The strategy worked, I guess. With one more round of walk-throughs with Mrs. Masmejean, most of our requests were granted. Mr. Sedes scowled.

For our final countdown we had all the usual suspects plus Ambassador Galbraith, General Counsel Homme, Charge Bill Barraclough, and Ty Cobb from the National Security Council. This was to be the "no-surprises" run through, but John Fisher had obviously spent the day being rolled and revealed endless cave-ins, which brought us all a good laugh.

We had a little cake for our WHCA lead, Hasdovick, at his last countdown.

## D DAY

Against all weather predictions, the sun came out again for Ronald Reagan. When I arrived at the entrance to the Parliament, I found Andrea Mitchell and Sam Donaldson in a confrontation with the VO and Secret Service. They were there to do live television broadcasts from the floor of the Parliament, but security would not admit them. Donaldson was screaming obscenities. Somebody had dropped the ball. Where were their passes? Where was Janet Anderson?

I walked up bearing such a dangling string of credentials for every conceivable area of the Parliament that I looked like a Brazilian Air Force General. I told the security people I would take personal responsibility for admitting them. Andrea Mitchell told me I was a "dreamboat." Donaldson just muttered under his breath.

Air Force One arrived on time. The president reviewed the honor guard in bright sunshine. I received regular updates by radio of the day's progress. Cathedral visit fine. Luncheon at the chateau fine. Mrs. Reagan's lunch at *Maison de Tanniers*, fine. Suddenly they were coming my way.

The motorcade arrived in the basement garage. We stepped into the elevators and I said, "Go." The operator threw the switch *and nothing happened.* The president glanced at me. "Go," I said again, as if ordering him more sternly would make a difference—we were all covered with flop sweat. But when the operator threw the switch a second time, we went.

Now Mr. Sedes got his revenge. I escorted President Reagan to a courtesy meeting with Pierre Pflimlin, president of the European Parliament. It had been agreed it would be just the two principals, no deputies, no press pool, just the two presidents onc-on-one. When we entered the elegant small room, we encountered Mr. Sedes, with a photographer and a videographer. Now it was my turn to scowl.

Our press would be irate if only the French side had a photo op. "Mr. Sedes," I hissed, "there were to be no photographers."

Mr. Sedes puffed up his chest and said, "In here, *I* give the orders."

I couldn't believe the arrogance. All the plans and discussions could simply be thrown out the window once he was in a position of control. I confronted the photographers and told them they would have to leave. They shrugged, pretending not to understand English. I hooked the two by the back of their collars, and dragged them over to the Secret Service agent at the door.

"Take these gentlemen into custody," I told the startled agent. The two Frenchmen suddenly regained their understanding of English and bolted for the hallway, as if pursued by the hounds of hell. The agent closed the door on them and beckoned me with his finger.

"I know," I said, "I'm sorry. I know you are not my private police force."

"Nice touch, though," the agent said, mimicking me, "Take these gentlemen into custody . . . "

Mr. Sedes himself was not supposed to be in the room, but I could do little about it. At least his sour expression gave me some satisfaction. I left the presidents to their parlay and Mr. Sedes to his fuming.

The president's address to the Parliament was now the final hurdle, and of course there was a glitch. About a third of the way through the speech, the teleprompter quit (WHCA's domain). Poor Hasdovick was apoplectic. His last trip and it became a WHCA fiasco. He was in the little cue room, the teleprompter motor burned out and shorting, trying to turn the drum by hand while being shocked, with Donald Regan and Mike Deaver shouting at him . . . quite a scene.

As it turned out, President Reagan continued with only a brief pause to switch to his script. Few in the hall even noticed.

Departure was flawless. As Air Force One lifted off, the rain began.

As I walked through the empty hemicycle (auditorium) to thank my volunteers, I encountered President Pflimlin. "Ah, Mr. Baxter, you should have a big smile for your wonderful event. You looked so glum up in the treaty room. Whatever was the matter?"

"Your Mr. Sedes is not an honorable man," I said, still irked at the memory of his actions.

"Why, of course not. He is a Turk."


The prefect had a grand reception for us, then a soiree hosted by the Alsatian food and wine industry, all quite delightful. Joel and Thierry were drunk and misty-eyed. Joel told me it had been "the most wonderful day of his life."

In the morning, our drivers were both waiting for us as we left the hotel for flights home, still proud to be "our team." Even though they were only paid through the day before, they insisted that we would not leave by taxi.

Joel and Thierry refused to leave before they saw us on our plane. In fact, they spoke to the gate agent and actually came onto the airplane before parting company, tears in eyes, with an Alsatian mug for each of us as a remembrance. Almost as soon as the plane lifted off, I began to crave foie gras—maybe knowing that I couldn't get the real thing made the growing taste for it more intense. When I changed planes in Paris, I found a little tin of "Alsatian foie gras" in the duty-free shop. After a big build-up, Pat and I opened it back home. It was awful. Dog food. I was so disappointed that I couldn't demonstrate the real delicacy, I called every French restaurant in Washington until I found one that flew in fresh foie gras terrines once a week.

Pat met me for a mid-week lunch date, where she finally understood what I had been talking about. We have been foie gras fans ever since.

\* \* \*

Joel came to visit us in America the next year. He stayed at the Baxter house and enjoyed several days touring Washington before he left to explore California.

After her safe return from France, Barbara Riggs, a noted horsewoman, fell off her own horse and missed several days of work. President Reagan sent her a book: *Principles of Horsemanship*.

Barbara Riggs became the first female deputy director of the United States Secret Service in 2004.

On a later trip, Walt McCay pushed the photo op privilege too far. Two gentlemen Walt recommended for photos with the president failed the criminal background checks and were rejected by the Secret Service. Walt was called on the carpet; he never did another presidential advance.

# CARIBBEAN CASTAWAYS

## ABOARD HAILSTONE

### 1986

In early 1986, when I had just turned forty, three GEICO executives had heart attacks over a single weekend. Two of the three died. All were forty or under. I told Pat, rather melodramatically, "This job is not worth dying for."

I began calculating how much money I had in investments and bank accounts. I found motivation on Monday mornings more difficult. On the way out the door one Monday, I said to Pat, casually, "We should sell the house, put the furniture in storage, and take the kids to the Caribbean on the boat before they are too old to go with us." I drove off to work.

Pat brooded all morning, before calling her brother, Ed. "You have to meet me for lunch. Terry has gone off the deep end."

Ed dropped everything, sensing a major crisis. Pat explained that I had suggested we sell the house, put the furniture in storage, and take the kids to the Caribbean.

Ed, bless his heart, said, "And the problem is?"

"Well it's goofy. Families don't just give up their homes and run off to the South Seas on a boat. It's too . . . well . . . irresponsible."

"A lot of people would, if they could," Ed countered. "It might be a great experience for your children."

Pat, her spirit of adventure challenged, went home thinking about education. Enterprisingly, she called the State Department to ask what they did for children posted with their parent overseas where the schools were not up to US standards.

She ended up with a page full of notes about the Calvert School, for junior high school levels, and the University of Nebraska for high school studies. Their correspondence programs were considered first-rate.

By the time I walked in that evening, whistling a happy tune, having forgotten my Monday morning blues, Pat had contacted each of the schools. She explained to me how we would solve the education dilemma. But my mind whispered, *Pat is on board, she has called my bluff.* We started actually thinking about my absurd idea.

The final shove came a couple of months later when Jack Byrne made the startling announcement that he was leaving GEICO to become the CEO of Fireman's Fund Insurance Company in California. He told me privately that he had signed a "no poaching" agreement, which meant he could not solicit any GEICO employees, say, me, for instance.

The spark went out of my business career in that instant. Boat plans moved to the front burner. Jack left GEICO in June; I left in July. Which is how Terry and Pat, eleven-year-old

Ashley, fourteen-year-old Bryan, and our family dog ended up on a forty-foot sailboat departing Annapolis.

Thanks to Mike Seligman, I had a book contract for my second novel, *The Ursa Ultimatum.* I had cranked out a quick hundred pages, but had never received the advance from the publisher. My inimitable agent, Audrey Wolf, said not to worry, she never had a publisher renege. Nevertheless, I stopped writing and started enjoying my family.

After years of being on the road, I now got to spend every waking hour with Pat and the children. It was heaven. I had been missing real life.

Our first mission was to see America, at the least the part that adjoined the East Coast. We were one of a hundred thousand boats in New York Harbor for the dedication of the refurbished Statue of Liberty—a Fourth-of-July celebration with tall ships, blimp races, the Blue Angels, fireworks, and fourteen of our closest friends from Washington all crammed on our tiny boat for the duration. The decks were covered with children in sleeping bags. What a start.

We visited Long Island Sound, Block Island, Newport, Martha's Vineyard, Kennebunkport, Boothbay Harbor, and Nantucket, among other ports and coves, before returning to Annapolis for boat service. While the boat was buffed, we drove out West to see the Tetons, the Grand Canyon, and Disneyland. We spent five wonderful days with Pat's sister in Los Angeles. Then, back across America by way of Texas, Nashville, and the Great Smokies. We made up for all the lost vacations.

Finally, we aimed *Hailstone* south, down the intercoastal waterway toward the Caribbean. "Hailstone" was the fictional

Secret Service code name for the vice president in my first book. Pat probably would have preferred *Lady Patricia,* or even *Summer Wind,* or any normal boat name, but, as always, she was agreeable and tolerant.

The intercoastal finally made us feel part of something. The annual migration of boats heading to winter sun was in full swing. We chatted with other boat owners while waiting for bridges to open and while docked in the marinas each night. Our shared ambitions made easy friendships. We began to notice other children. "I can't believe there are other families as goofy as we are," Pat said, beginning to feel more normal. Ashley and Bryan sought out other children each stop, and before long the kids were herding the adults into the same destinations. For the next couple of years, we had a flotilla of four boats with children of similar ages to share our adventures.

Christmas in Charleston, New Year's in Hilton Head, and a long meander through the Abacos and the Exumas. Sunny skies, beach barbeques, fish fries, snorkeling, and crystal clear waters. What was not to love?

By the time we arrived in Providenciales in the Turks and Caicos, hurricane season was approaching. I also at long last received the advance payment for my book, just as Audrey promised. The only problem was I hadn't written a word in nine months, and the manuscript was now due in four months. We decided to stay put in Provo's Turtle Cove while I slaved away at my laptop.

Jack Alberschardt was the proprietor of the Turtle Cove Yacht Club where we perched for four months. Most of our other friends went on to the Virgin Islands, but we had a grand time in Provo. The club had a pool, tennis courts, and a terrific restaurant where the chef, Alfred, made delectable sweetbreads. Alberschardt, a gregarious Welshman, had his first Scotch at five o'clock, which would move him to songs, stories, and free drinks for his companions. I was a frequent companion.

Jack was a frustrated novelist. When he heard I was working on a book on my boat, he said, "Come into my air-conditioned office. We can work on our laptops back to back and inspire each other." So I did. He had his alter ego, Charlie Tipton, to rescue Provo from the corrupt drug trade. I had my determination to save the world from certain disaster in my suspense thriller. We passed many hours chuckling at our own prose until the magic hour of five o'clock was its own reward.

I was glad to be in the well-protected Turtle Cove basin when Hurricane Emily scored a direct hit. I spent a long night on the boat, adjusting lines to meet the changing winds. Pat and the children were snug in Alfred's restaurant while I ate cold beans from a can.

Hundreds of miles away, in Washington, D.C., my mother watched on television as Hurricane Emily struck the Turks and Caicos. She had no way to reach us; our local phone service had been out for hours. She did what any mother would do: she called her congressman. "My son is in the Turks and Caicos and a hurricane just went over," she told the poor intern who answered.

"What would you have us do, Madame?"

"I don't know. *You're* the government."

The next day, we were gathered in the bar, telling each other how brave we had been, when two gigantic West Indian policemen walked in. "We're looking for Terry Baxter," they announced loudly.

Everyone looked at me. The policemen followed the eyes to my barstool and asked, "Are you Terry Baxter?"

The room was hushed. Was I about to be deported? "Yes," I said weakly.

The bigger policeman crossed his arms and eyed me sternly. "Your mother called the ambassador. The ambassador called the chief of police. The chief of police called us, and now *you* are going to call your mother." Amid laughter and catcalls, they marched me to the bar phone.

My mother was overjoyed to hear my voice. The entire bar was making wind noises in the background. "Mom," I said above the maelstrom, "the storm is past. Everyone is safe. Please don't call the United Nations."


In early November, with a favorable weather window, we set sail for Puerto Rico and the Virgin Islands. Jack Alberschardt escorted us all the way out to the pass in his runabout to wish us fair winds. "Send me a book," he shouted as we drew away. I would miss him.

We had a glorious reunion with our boat friends in the Virgins. As 1986 turned into 1987, we enjoyed a series of visits from our shorebound friends up north. Ron Hamway, the hero of the inaugural gala, brought his family for a week, along with a five-pound Virginia ham, which lasted a month even in the warm climate. We toured all of the island delights: Soper's Hole, Foxy's, the Last Resort, The Bitter End Yacht Club, and found all the little out-of-the-way anchorages the bareboats never discovered. No amount of money could buy the experience we were having with our children.

But as 1987 moved from summer into fall, Ashley and Bryan were beginning to wonder what they were missing back in civilization. Ashley had never "changed classes," for instance (evidently one of the attractions of high school versus grade school; who knew?), and Bryan was certain he was missing the "cool songs." (Every island band had a repertoire of two songs: "Lady in Red" and "Hot, Hot, Hot.") I always thought of the trip as "three to five years." Pat thought, "one." Now we had been voyaging for almost two years.

Once again, external events helped us decide. I got a message from my mail-forwarding service that the White House was trying to reach me. I called from Tortola. Could I come to Washington to talk about a White House job? Well, yes I could, but I didn't have any real clothes, just cut-offs and flip-flops. Just come as you are, they said, and we'll worry about clothes later.

. . . Which is how I arrived in wintery Washington, D.C., with a bright tan and island clothes. When I presented myself at the White House gate, they examined me suspiciously. Who could blame them?

"Do you have an appointment?" the Secret Service agent asked dubiously.

"Yes." I gave them my name. He seemed surprised that I did, indeed, appear to have an appointment.

"You need a photo ID."

"I have a passport," I said, and tried to open my briefcase, the type that has the three little dials to set a lock code. One latch opened fine. The other refused to budge. I never used the locks, but I realized in dread that I had somehow nudged the dial, which reset the code.

"What seems to be the problem?" the guard demanded.

"Well, somehow I've reset the combination . . ."

His hand moved to his holster. "What is the combination?"

I stammered now. "It's not the combination, see, the one side opens fine . . ."

Now he stepped back and said more loudly, "*What* is the combination?"

I was forced to admit that the combination to my briefcase, on a lock I never used, was "007."

In spite of himself he broke into loud laughter. He picked up the phone and said, "Get me some back-up here. I've got a guy dressed in flip-flops, locked himself out of his briefcase," he couldn't stop his pitch from rising and his voice filling with humor, "and he thinks he's James Bond."

In thirty seconds I was surrounded by smirking Secret Service agents. After hearing a recitation of events, the lead agent asked, "Sir, may we break open your briefcase lock?"

"Yes, of course. Please do."

He used a small hammer to knock off the latch. With a flood of relief, I pointed to my passport. After some good-natured ribbing, I was sent on my way.

For the next two years, whenever I entered the White House, one or another of the agents would be there to intone, "Bond, *James* Bond."

I met with James C. Miller III, the director of the Office of Management and Budget (OMB). We liked each other right away, in spite of my less than optimum appearance. He was direct and to the point. "Look, Terry, it's the last year of the Reagan administration. It's hard to get top people to give up a career when they know the president can't be reelected. Then they told me this great guy, Baxter, was floating around the Caribbean somewhere, and could start next week if he wanted to. So, will you?"

He must have realized he cut to the chase too abruptly, because he began to smooth it in with his Southern charm. "You may not know about OMB, nobody does. It is the Executive Office of the President. Every act of Congress comes to us to analyze, every veto threat is initiated by us, and every departmental budget is approved by us. We are the largest policy office in the White House. I am a member of the President's Cabinet. You will be assistant director of OMB, an official member of the White House staff—you must certainly want that after all the work you've done. George Shultz was director of OMB, now he is secretary of state. Casper Weinberger was head of OMB, now he is secretary of defense. One of my deputies was just selected to be ambassador to NATO. This is where it happens. OMB is the principal power center of the White House, it's the point of the lance."

It was a great speech. I was breathless. I reached out and shook his hand.

I flew back to Tortola to tell Pat we were going home. We made arrangements with the dock master to look after the boat—I would have to return for *Hailstone* later. Pat would take some time to close everything up, and then come back to

Washington to find a home. I left the next day after a tearful farewell party from our assorted boat mates.

What our children would later call "the great adventure of their lives" was over. We would remember the serenity of a secluded anchorage with nothing but the ghosts of rum-runners, or the screaming gale we named "hurricane bimbo," but, most of all, we would remember the friends we made along the way and the treasured moments of being a family together.

* * *

A year and a half later, I got a telegram from Jack Alberschardt inviting me to the book party for his new novel *The Provo Affair,* at the Turtle Cove Yacht Club. I was unable to attend, but I ordered a bottle of champagne from Alfred's and sent my congratulations. Jack told me later that the locals enjoyed his free booze and hors d'oeuvres, then went home to read their free novel where Charlie Tipton battles the corruption and drugs in Provo. The locals began to recognize themselves in the book and were not flattered. They returned in the middle of the night in a rage.

The small mob broke the windows out of the yacht club while Jack and his family hid in the hotel. They set his pick-up truck on fire. Eventually the police came to escort the Alberschardts to the airport. Jack flew to Miami, sold his interest in the yacht club to his partners, and never returned to Provo. All because we shared his office to inspire each other. . . . We shared more than a few five-o'clock sunsets back in the states before he passed away.

Every Christmas, we receive cards from boating families scattered from Canada (*Prairie Sailor)* to the Antilles (*Ayacora*). Great memories, all.

GEICO, after unburdening itself of the overhead of Jack Byrne and Terry Baxter, went on to become one of the premier insurance companies in America under the impeccable leadership of Tony Nicely.

# WHITE HOUSE STAFFER

I went to a men's shop and told them I wanted four suits if they could alter them by the end of the day. They could. I bought shirts as well as actual shoes (instead of flip-flops) and ties. While the flip-flops were retired, my deep tan took longer to shed.

My friend, Jim Handlon, offered me his spare room in McLean, Virginia, until Pat could return to find us a home. Jim was such a great host and fabulous chef that I became "the guest who wouldn't leave." Pat brought the kids back and settled in her family's vacation cottage in Pennsylvania while she searched Northern Virginia for a place to live. We reentered civilization with hardly a look back.

OMB was located in the Old Executive Office Building (EOB), part of the White House complex. Staff spent half the day walking back and forth for various meetings and briefings. Also in the EOB were the Advance Office, the Military Office of the White House, the Council of Economic Advisors, and the Office of the Vice President, among others. Even after more than a decade of visits, it was a thrill to walk the corridors as an employee.

It was fun to drop into the Advance Office, which had been little more than the other end of a telephone for years. Our lifeline in the Advance Office had been Joanne Hildebrand. She juggled the assignments, calmed the tantrums, and invariably solved any logistical problems we could test her with. Her steady hand was a welcome refuge in the frequent chaos.

Now I could put faces with other names. Shelby Scarbrough I already knew, but Lisa Walker and Ashley Parker only had been cheerful voices until now. Ashley, in particular, as "contact central" had helped me solve so many problems, we felt like old friends who were seeing each other for the first time.

Returning from a Christmas visit to California, Ashley brought me a bottle of wine from her family's vineyard. I studied the bottle of Crockett's Reserve.

"Where does 'Crockett' come from if your wine is Parker Vineyards?" I asked.

Ashley looked at me as if I had dropped in from Mars. "Oh, I guess you don't know. My father is Fess Parker. Maybe Davy Crockett was before your time . . ."

I laughed. No, Davy Crockett was *not* before my time. Just like every other twelve-year-old boy in America, I could remember all the verses of "The Ballad of Davy Crockett." I began to whistle the tune.

"Stop now," Ashley ordered sternly, "before I have to scalp you."

OMB was a great assignment. Just as I sensed in our first meeting, Jim Miller became a close friend and generously inclusive boss. Within weeks, we were finishing each other's sentences. Somewhere inside, Jim wanted to be a crusading Southern senator, pounding the gavel in televised hearings. His aw-shucks, good-ol'-boy emerged with his Southern drawl when he gave a speech. But he loved his position at OMB. We always knew when he was back from the morning staff meetings, because he was preceded by a cacophony of echoing footsteps, snapping fingers, and a happy whistle. He was a contented man in motion.

The weeks passed in a blizzard of economic briefings, Sunday morning television appearances, speeches, and staff meetings. Jim and I managed a short overseas swing through our embassies in Paris and London to brief the foreign press. After a long day in Paris, we both fell into beds in our embassy's guest rooms. When I awoke, I noticed my bed had a plaque. I got my glasses out to read it:

> "On the night of May 21, 1927, in this bed, Charles Lindbergh spent his first night in Paris after his historic flight from Roosevelt Field, New York, to Le Bourget, Paris."

I called Jim and said, "You've got to see this."

"You slept in Lindbergh's bed," he exclaimed as he read it. We rushed back to his more palatial suite and scrutinized the bed for plaques. Nothing. I think Jim was honestly miffed that he had such an ordinary bed.

In May, Jim Hooley asked if I could advance the president's welcome home from the Moscow summit. Air Force One would fly into Andrews Air Force Base, and Hooley wanted my usual brass band and bleacher celebration. Jim Miller had said, of course, I should do it.

Advance work back in Washington was now a special treat. I was in home territory. I could invite my friends to participate, I could sleep in my own bed, and I could reunite with some of my favorite colleagues. Andrews was a particularly plum assignment, because, one, I could use Mark Rosenker for press, and Mark "owned" press arrangements at Andrews, and two, I would have a full complement of military personnel to assist with the set-up, and they were seasoned pros. Most important, the Air Force One Advance Team assured me they could accomplish my special surprise.

My site was a hangar on the base. The arrival I visualized was for Air Force One to taxi up outside the hangar, which I had converted into a three-sided indoor amphitheater crammed with bleachers and bands. Just when the crowd inside would expect Air Force One to park as usual and the president to emerge, I wanted the plane to turn sharply into the hangar until the entire nose had thrust into the center of the crowd.

It was a stunning effect. Some in the audience actually worried the pilot didn't realize the hangar was occupied, but the nose wheel came to rest exactly where the Air Force One advance team had promised. The guests broke into relieved and enthusiastic applause when the engines were cut. Hooley, who was with the president onboard, told me Reagan had looked tired and worn after a grueling summit and long flight, but when he saw the cheering well-wishers in stands reaching to the rafters, he said, "Wow, just look at that."

"That crowd was an elixir," Hooley said.

Jim Miller was like the father of the bride. He hosted other members of the Cabinet on the South Lawn of the White House, where they boarded a helicopter for the short ride to Andrews. I had reserved a special VIP section for them just in front of the podium. Like a proud papa, Jim made a show of introducing me to each of his colleagues. White House staff and guests had arrived by bus.

The president and Mrs. Reagan and the vice president and Mrs. Bush waved from the door of the plane amid the cheering spectators, then took seats on the platform. Reagan delivered a brief summary of his hopes for the summit and expressed how wonderful it was to be home with such a warm welcome from his staff.

Watching from the side of the platform, I saw my beaming guest, Bill Scott, my teammate from when we raced cars together twenty years before, sitting next to the secretary of the treasury in my reserved VIP section. Another moment that money couldn't buy.

Later that week, I got a call from Joe Canzeri. He asked me to meet him at the Bush for President offices across town. Joe explained that he was going to run the campaign for the vice presidential candidate and he wanted me to be the head of advance. I was honored by his confidence in me and excited at the prospect of working together again.

"Who is the candidate?" I asked.

"I don't know. It won't be decided until the convention."

"Let me talk it over with Jim Miller," I said.

Joe nodded. "I'll hold it open for you, but not for long."

Jim Miller was immediately negative. In fact, he acted hurt that I would consider jumping ship. Early in our tenure together, Jim had confessed he would probably leave before the end of the president's term, which would free me to join Bush's campaign if I wanted to. But now, seven months later, Jim was still firmly in place. "I'm not ready to go," he said. "I need you here."

I was pleased that Jim cared. Being wanted by two of your favorite people is a high-class problem to have. Of course, I would stay.

"Besides," Jim said, "I am really doing you a favor. If you work the veep candidate, you'd probably end up on the vice president's staff. Is that what you want?"

It was a very good question. I wasn't very strategic in my career planning. I just had faith that if I did my best, good things would happen. But, Jim helped me realize that the vice president's staff was not my goal. I had noticed how George Bush's staff, good people all, were clearly second-class citizens in the Reagan White House. Just as an example, only the chief of staff to the vice president had White House Mess privileges, while all of the senior staff at OMB did. I was sure that slights large and small must chafe after a while.

I told Joe Canzeri I was sorry, but Jim Miller wasn't ready to let me go. I found out shortly that I had narrowly dodged a bullet. Dan Quayle was unveiled as the vice presidential candidate early in the week of the Republican convention. Jim

Miller and I watched on television as Quayle leaped on stage as if launched from a jack-in-the-box. Quayle's manic introduction caused Jim to say, "You can thank me later."

Jim and I were in New Orleans to act as "surrogates," high and mid-level administration figures who would meet with delegates' caucuses to schmooze and inspire them. Jim circulated with a panel made up of Clarence Thomas, EEOC director, and Olympia Snow, senator from Maine. They each recounted interesting personal stories and provided background on various issues of the day. We were "eyes and ears" for the convention staff and made ourselves available to the press for color commentary. Jim was in his element.

In the meantime, the media was shredding Dan Quayle. His service in the National Guard was hotly debated, and his responses were less than inspiring. Joe Canzeri's blood pressure was surely in overdrive.

On the night the candidate for vice president was to be formally nominated, Jim and I were on the convention floor, giving supportive interviews for Dan Quayle. A runner took us aside and said, "No more Quayle interviews." The same message was passed to other surrogates on the floor. We were left in limbo for the next forty-five minutes.

My theory was that the power brokers gathered behind the stage were trying to find some way out of a Quayle nomination, but it was too late. That night J. Danforth Quayle was officially nominated to be vice president of the United States.

Back in Washington, I was called up one more time to do President Reagan's last address to the United Nations. New York

City with Grey Terry, rooms in the Waldorf Astoria, backstage at the United Nations, and to top it off, Jim Hooley scheduled me on Air Force One for the trip home.

While the events at the United Nations were historic and well-reported, the biggest moment came backstage at the Waldorf, unseen, and fortunately, not historic.

The day after his eloquent United Nations speech on disarmament, President Reagan was meeting with a series of heads-of-state in "bilaterals," one-on-one meetings in Suite 35H of the Waldorf Astoria. The visiting prime ministers and presidents were waiting in suites arrayed along the corridor. The entire floor was secure.

One at a time, I would bring the vistors down the hall to 35H, where the two heavy doors were open to reveal a welcoming Ronald Reagan. Two chairs, two country's flags, a fifteen- or twenty-minute meeting. Mark Wienberg, a press office aide, would bring the press from the visiting country to the thirty-fifth floor by elevator for a photo op, then the doors would close. While the meeting took place, we prepared the next flag and the next visitor.

About halfway through the schedule, I had just delivered a prime minister. The president and the prime minister were comfortably seated in front of the flag backdrop. In the stairway next to the elevator, I heard the pounding of feet. Then I heard a loud angry voice.

"Hey. Hey! Stop! Halt!"

The heavy footfalls were closer. "Stop or I'll shoot!" The voice was now frenzied. "Take cover!"

I had only a second to turn toward the door twenty feet away when it burst open. Mark Wienberg stumbled out with a New York policeman around his shoulders tackling him. The policeman held a gun to the back of Wienberg's head. "Who are you, you motherfucker," the policeman screamed.

President Reagan leaned forward curiously, a little "O" on his lips. Glen Smith, the Secret Service agent in 35H, slammed the suite doors shut.

My expression pretty much mirrored the president's. I realized later, if this had been a terrorist attack, I would have offered nothing more than a juicy target. So much for race-driver reflexes.

In time, tensions subsided and the story emerged. The press elevator had jammed. Mark Wienberg had run up thirty-five stories to deliver the news. The police officer had not recognized Mark's White House pin. Mark was too exhausted to speak. Chaos ensued.

Agent Glen Smith later said, "If I'd had a clear shot at the man, I would have shot him." A close thing.

\* \* \*

Now, as Frank Sinatra would say, it was the autumn of our years. Jim Miller announced he was leaving OMB. Bush's campaign for the presidency was in the final week, and I did my last advance for President Reagan.

The site was the National War College on the grounds of Ft. McNair in downtown Washington. Ft. McNair is the headquarters of the US Army Military District of Washington, and therefore home to the many officers who assisted on inaugurations and other special events over the years. It was a nice place to finish.

On the other side of the green from where the president would speak, grim history had been made. In the earliest example of photojournalism, Alexander Gardner captured the execution of the Lincoln conspirators on July 7, 1865.

In our last countdown meeting, the WHCA lead told me the president had twice jumped the intro recently. The standard introduction sequence was four bars of "Ruffles and Flourishes," then the WHCA announcement, "Ladies and gentlemen, the President of the United States" (which is the cue), then "Hail to the Chief" as the president enters. In the last two events, the president had entered when he heard "Ruffles and Flourishes."

This is what led me to unconsciously take the president's elbow as we stood at the entrance. I was concentrating intently on my schedule.

The president gave me THE LOOK and said, "It's all right, I won't go until you tell me."

It was only when he looked down at his arm that I realized I was gripping him. I recoiled in horror at my faux pas.

The president walked out with a jaunty smile at my reaction.

\* \* \*

We gave Jim Miller an affectionate farewell party where we sang a "Capitol Steps"-style anthem to the tune of "You Picked a Fine Time to Leave Me, Lucille."

You picked a fine time to leave OMB

With pork barrel programs, a real spending spree.

Congress has fought you,

Thought they out-thought you,
But you showed them that no lunch is free,
You picked a fine time to leave OMB.
They run for the coffers, they make you lewd offers,
They're always advancing a plea.
Those agency budgets, looming above us,
Like ink in a rising red sea.
But you kept resisting, kept the ship from listing,
So we'll always remember with glee,
That we were the cutters, the budget rebutters,
That shared in your great legacy.

Jim Miller had been part of the Reagan administration from day one. He was the first administrator of the Office of Information and Regulatory Affairs. Then from 1981 to 1985 he was the chairman of the Federal Trade Commission, and finally the director of the United States Office of Management and Budget—from mid-level appointee to a member of the President's Cabinet in the stretch of two terms. I was proud to be one of the friends and colleagues who helped him across the finish line.

The president addressed us in the conference room and said at the end, "Jim will become a distinguished fellow at the Center for the Study of Public Policy at George Mason University, and distinguished fellow for Citizens for a Sound Economy, and chairman of an advisory board to Washington Economic Research Consultant. He calls this taking a break . . . Godspeed and God bless you, Jim."

\* \* \*

Joe Canzeri had a perfectly miserable campaign. After a series of early gaffes, Quayle was relegated to small states and insignificant appearances. Joe said his main mission was "to keep Quayle out of sight and away from the press as much as possible." A thankless task.

George H. W. Bush and Dan Quayle carried forty states and won 426 electoral votes and 53.4 percent of the vote in 1988.

I often thought about that policeman from the Waldorf in New York City. Standing alone all day in the stairwell of the thirty-fourth floor, then a moment of sheer terror as Wienberg sprinted up the stairs at him. In a split second, he might decide his entire future, and his own or others' lives. If he had shot Mark Wienberg, his career would be over in disgrace. If he admitted an intruder that led to an assassination, his career would be over in disgrace. Somehow, he navigated a middle ground with no permanent injuries. Well done.

After President Reagan left the White House, Joanne Hildebrand-Drake ran his California office with the same skill she brought to the Advance Office, which is to say *perfectly*. She went on to be the chief administrative officer for the Ronald Reagan Presidential Foundation.

Mark Rosenker created one of the most impressive careers of any of us out of his advance experiences. He became a lead in the George W. Bush campaign shortly after the debates. After the election, he became the head of the Military Office of the White House, a plum position in charge of Air Force One operations and WHCA, among other responsibilities. He was with President Bush on 9/11, and it was Mark who implemented the continuity of government order. He told me he saw history before his eyes. "I watched the president transform from a peacetime CEO of the executive branch to one who assumed the awesome responsibilities of commander-in-chief in a single day. Bush was resolute, focused, and committed to justice whatever it took." Mark later became the chairman of NTSB, after hearing from me that it was the best job in government. He achieved the rank of major general in the United States Air Force.

In the last week of his presidency, Ronald Reagan inscribed my photo from Air Force One, "Dear Terry 'One Punch' Baxter— My appreciation for all you've done, and warm regards."

To the great relief of Jim Handlon, who had shared his house with me for most of a year, Pat discovered a small historic farm near Charlottesville, Virginia, where I began to contemplate becoming an unemployed grape farmer.

# The American Bicentennial
# Presidential Inaugural Gala

Joe Canzeri was resurrected from the Siberia of the Quayle campaign to be the chairman of the inaugural gala once more. His first phone call was to me. This time we were working with Don Mischer, David Goldberg, and Bill Bracken as producers, and Walter Miller as director. I missed Michael Seligman, but it was a great team.

For introducers, we had Chuck Yeager, Arnold Schwarzenegger, Chuck Norris, Clint Eastwood, Cheryl Ladd, and Walter Cronkite. The talent was skewed to country performers, Bush's favorites: Randy Travis, the Oak Ridge Boys, Loretta Lynn, and Crystal Gayle, but we also had Yo-Yo Ma, Anita Baker, Mikhail Baryshnikov, Nell Carter, Julio Iglesias, Tommy Tune, and Frank Sinatra. Also returning was our favorite juggler, Michael Davis, and we planned a special surprise performance, not even listed in the program.

I also had learned the Gatlin Brothers were returning to perform at another inaugural venue, which gave me the opportunity to include them as guests in my box for the gala.

The site came together quickly, since we could basically reproduce our set-up from 1985. We again opened the dress rehearsal to White House staff, which allowed me to entertain all my colleagues from OMB, a happy opportunity.

The executive director for the Inaugural Committee was Steve Studdert, my old co-worker from the Ford Press Advance Office. He was, as always, decisive and supportive. The inaugural group director in charge of the gala preparations was Bill Harris. Bill was new to me, but I appreciated his direct management style and his guiding principles: "maintain an even strain," and "always show grace under pressure." We spent many evenings sharing philosophy over Scotch and cigars after my weekly gala updates, and became good friends.

So, to say the build-up to the gala went smoothly is an understatement. However, Murphy always knows a disaster is lurking. Incredibly, it would be tickets again.

*Ghost of Colonel Klink.*

The day before the final dress rehearsal, Joe and I were called near midnight. Steve Studdert wanted to see us at the convention center right away. Joe and I arrived to find Steve with Ron Kaufman, the National Republican committeeman from Massachusetts. Steve was studying the convention center blueprints I had sent him, not a good sign.

"Okay," said Studdert, "here's the problem. The gala is sold out."

Canzeri and I looked at each other. This was a problem?

Then Kaufman explained in his thick Boston accent, which made it hard to understand, "No one pulled my tickets for the National Committee people."

Studdert was looking around the performance hall. "We need more seats. Can we move one of these walls back?"

Canzeri looked at me.

"Can't do it," I said.

"No one ever said that to me," Studdert shot back, "and lived."

I smiled. It was a good line. Studdert was like Canzeri: his face often appeared deadpan, but if you looked closely, you often detected the hint of humor in his eyes. Tonight there was no hint.

But I knew Steve often went for some impossible solution so the very difficult solution would seem better. I tried to nudge the discussion in the direction of "very difficult." So I explained, "We just spent the whole day yesterday doing the final sound check—the whole day and a hundred thousand dollars. We don't have time to move any walls and repeat the acoustical testing. We're talking about a live television broadcast in less than twenty-four hours."

I turned to Ron Kaufman. "How many seats do you need?"

"One hundred. Two per state."

A hundred seats! *Maintain grace under pressure.* I slowly scanned the room. "Okay," I said, imagining the fire marshal again, "here's what I can do. I can put two seats at the end of each row on this aisle," I pointed, "and this aisle." I snapped open my briefcase and opened the box of my unused business cards from the Inaugural Committee. I started writing on the back of each one "A01, A02, B01, B02" and so on.

Studdert, always pushing, said, "What if four want to sit together?"

"Ron can give out four together, but they'll have to sit two by two." I continued to write seat numbers. "But, you can tell your VIPs that this aisle," I pointed again, "is where the president and the performers will enter, so they will be right in the heart of the action, and the other aisle is where the celebrity hosts will speak, so those seats will be among the stars. I'll tell my ushers and ticket checkers to be on the lookout for these extras."

Ron Kaufman was smiling. He had arrived expecting the worst, but I had rescued him.

If Kaufman was happy, Studdert was happy. "All right. Thanks."

Joe Canzeri gave me his deadpan look, but in his eyes I *could* see the humor. After that night, Joe called me "Sir Galahad." I called him, with great affection, "the dwarf wop."


The next morning's crisis was from my new friend Bill Harris. His office was in charge of dispensing the passes for each event to admit non-ticket holders like performers and caterers. I had not received my allotment at the end of the day before, as promised. The Secret Service sweep of the convention center was underway. Once it was completed, musicians and talent would start arriving for the dress rehearsal. Harris was unavailable.

I told my staff to print our own passes and be ready to distribute them. I went to Bill Harris' office. "I thought I might see you," he said, unruffled. "There's no way we are giving you six hundred and sixty passes. What are you trying to pull?"

I tried to keep the annoyance out of my voice. This was exactly the kind of bureaucratic nonsense I detested. "Bill, I'm not trying to pull anything. I've only asked for what I need. Add it up yourself. I have a hundred ushers, twenty coat-check people, a hundred and thirty performers, TV crew, and orchestra, then three hundred and sixty for the Mormon Tabernacle Choir alone, then the Naval Academy Glee Club, and the caterers . . ."

"A hundred ushers?" he said, seizing on my first number. "You've got to be kidding."

*Maintain an even strain.* "Bill," I said calmly, "I have twelve thousand patrons arriving, who need to promptly find their seats so we can start a *live* television broadcast. That's a single usher for each one hundred and twenty people."

"Make me a list and we'll talk about it."

"I don't have time for more talk. I have performers arriving in an hour. I should have had the passes last night. You are not leaving me much choice. I'll have to issue my own passes if you can't provide what I need."

His eyes bulged. He stood and walked out. I watched him go in the next office. Was he dismissing me? Was he conferring with someone? I waited five minutes. Then I stood. It would take me twenty minutes to get back to the convention center. I had to go.

Harris walked back in with a box of passes. "If I find out you are screwing me . . ."

I took the box. "I am not screwing you, Bill. I'm just trying to do the job. And you are not making it easy."

The show was great. Pat and I enjoyed our evening with the Gatlins. There were a couple of glitches that only an insider would notice. One female headliner refused to answer her stage call. "She's not ready yet," the hapless stagehand said to director Walter Miller by intercom. Miller exploded, "Does Miss Prima Donna realize this is a live show?"

"She's not ready," the stagehand repeated lamely.

Miller recued the orchestra and went to the next act. More magnanimous than I would have been, he worked her into the program later.

Frank Sinatra had rehearsed two songs. Whether he would actually perform one song, or two, depended upon how the show was running on timing. Walter Miller confirmed by intercom, "One song, one song."

I suspect Sinatra thought he could force the second song. After his first number, he turned to the orchestra leader and said, "Maestro . . ."

As the director had instructed, the orchestra leader had already cued up the next performer's music. He held his hands out helplessly at Sinatra.

"That's what you got for me?" Sinatra abruptly dropped his microphone on the stage and walked off. Walter Miller cut to commercial. The incident was edited out for the Central and Western time zones, but Eastern viewers must have scratched their heads.

Our unscheduled surprise was a smash hit. Joe's wife, Tricia, had suggested a number from the new hit Broadway show *Phantom of the Opera*. Everyone agreed the Thursday night presidential gala would conflict with the cast's New York performance schedule, but Tricia pursued it. She is a persuasive woman. The two lead stars agreed to take a night off to perform for the president.

So, with no celebrity introduction, no listing in the program, just a mysterious fog spreading across the stage, followed by the shattering organ music, *The Phantom*, Michael Crawford emerged by trapdoor, rising into the mist to sing "The Music of the Night." Nothing short of spectacular.

We drove home to our little farm in Charlottesville, happy, exhausted, and unemployed.

* * *

I'm not sure if Bill Harris ever concluded that I played it straight with him, but if not, I hope he reads this. Bill, I never skimmed a single pass. Bill remains the go-to guy for Republican conventions and inaugurals.

Ron Kaufman had every justification to take credit for saving the gala seats for his political team. Instead he hewed to one of Ronald Reagan's best aphorisms: *It's amazing what you can accomplish when you don't care who gets the credit.* Ron let the participants know that the business card that held their seat numbers on the back was from the guy who saved the day. After the event, I received nearly thirty letters of thanks and praise for the gala. To say I had warm feelings is an understatement.

Ron Kaufman became White House political director for George H. W. Bush, and a political heavyweight for decades to come.

# Saving NBW

After two weeks of planting grapevines in Virginia and relaxing, it was time to retrieve our sailboat, *Hailstone,* from the Caribbean. I recruited five of my best friends to meet me in Tortola for the *Hailstone* rescue mission: Ron Hamway, Ben Beattie, Phil Haseltine, Chuck Hurley, and John Gregory.

To make their sacrifice worthwhile, I planned to spend four or five days in paradise. Time to see the wonders of the British Virgins and to become familiar with the boat. Chuck immediately confessed that visiting the Virgins was his real objective for the trip, and perhaps he would skip the twelve hundred miles of open water to make landfall in the US mainland. This was fair. Chuck worked as hard as anyone to help prepare the boat and created the lion's share of the fun. He was good company, but we allotted him the worst bunk for his treachery.

I got a late call from Cliff Ehrlich, a business colleague from Marriott. An ocean voyage in a sailboat was on his bucket list. Was there still time to join us? Since Chuck was planning to depart on our last day in Tortola, I told Cliff he could slip in, but I was sorry he missed the fun of the Baths, the Bitter End, Jost Van Dyke, and Norman Island.

We sailed to St. Thomas on the US side to drop off Chuck and pick up Cliff. Chuck was the life of the party, so it was hard to let him go. Cliff inherited the worst bunk. He arrived in a blue blazer and Bass weejuns. He was pumped, but I worried that the reality of open water would be a wake-up call for him.

It was, for all of us.

We left St. Thomas as the sun was setting. We turned north after skirting the bottom of the island. Now we had eight hundred miles of ocean separating us from the lower Bahamas, about a week of day-and-night sailing.

It was February, usually a calm period. But the winds and the waves started building in the first hour after darkness. Soon towering breakers were sweeping across us from the northeast. Ron and Ben were huddled with me in the cockpit. John, Cliff, and Phil were braced in their bunks down below. We shortened sail several times until only a reefed main and triangle of jib remained, but the wind continued to howl. Cliff poked his head out of the companionway to ask, "Is it always like this?"

Ron, Ben, and I laughed. No, this was bad. I decided to turn downwind to head for San Juan, Puerto Rico. The ride was better, but we still had hours of flying spray and breaking seas. Ben called them "kickers" and "shit kickers." Nothing like the pleasant sail I had enjoyed on the trip south.

When we finally approached San Juan, the seas grew steeper as we neared the channel past El Morro. The huge seas swept us toward the harbor with minimal control. Just then, the Coast

Guard called to advise us to "stand off." A freighter in distress was already in the harbor entrance.

John Gregory came to life below to answer the radio. "Negative, negative. We are coming in," he said grimly. In truth, we probably had no choice. To attempt a turn into the breaking rollers would have probably swamped us. We fought to stay clear of the freighter, but we were both corks in a bathtub.

At last, behind the protection of the fortress, the wind and waves abated. We sloshed wetly into the lee. The sudden calm made it hard to imagine the maelstrom just outside. Dog tired, we motored into the harbor and dropped anchor. Everything was soaked in seawater, but we were safe. We fell into the soggy beds without another word.

Cliff Ehrlich's first night at sea in a sailboat was not the idyll he had imagined.

It took three days for the storm to blow out. We heard they had recorded seventy-four mile per hour winds at the airport—a near hurricane. In February! Three boats were lost off the coast.

We brought everything on deck to dry out. John and Cliff sensibly decided their wives and sweethearts needed them at home more than we did on the boat. On our last day together, we toured El Morro. We looked out at the channel we had entered. "Still white caps," Phil pointed out. The park ranger who overheard us said, "That's nothing. You should have seen it three days ago."

"We did. We came in three nights ago."

"You're the sailboat that came in?" the ranger said in wonder. "Must have been some ride."

We replaced all the food, bid farewell to John and Cliff, and set off again the next day. After a week of glorious sun, magical sunsets, and endless retelling of our harrowing "hurricane" exploits, Ben, Ron, Phil, and Terry arrived in Georgetown in the Exumas. Time constraints caught up with Ron and Ben in spite of our now pleasant adventure, and they each caught island flights home. Phil and I soldiered on to Nassau, where Phil also had to return to work. The only unemployed shipmate, I sailed the last hundred miles on my own, with fond memories of the excitement we had shared. *Hailstone* was back in home waters.

\* \* \*

Back in Washington, I began thinking of work. A GEICO colleague reconnected me with Luther Hodges, CEO of the National Bank of Washington. I knew and liked Luther on a social level. We had jointly shepherded several charitable events over the years. Now, he and the bank were in a fight for their lives.

The NBW story deserved a book of its own, with its dreary tale of intrigue from the Middle East and multiple failures of bank regulators, but I was only part of the final struggle for boardroom control in 1989.

The National Bank of Washington was the Capitol's oldest bank. It financed the construction of the Washington Monument. But, by the seventies, the bank had fallen on hard times under corrupt ownership. The comptroller of the Currency was trying to broker a sale to better stewards. Enter Luther Hodges. An experienced banker from North Carolina and the scion of a political dynasty—his father had been governor of

North Carolina and secretary of commerce under JFK—Luther was deputy secretary of commerce for Jimmy Carter, and had been a respected banker with a squeaky-clean record. Luther was encouraged to assemble investors to buy NBW.

Unfortunately for the future of the bank, about a quarter of the money came from Saudi Arabia by way of investor Wafic Saïd. In time the relationship soured. Saïd claimed Hodges was not delivering satisfactory profits. Hodges claimed Saïd was interfering in internal bank matters and complained to regulators. By the time I arrived at the door, suits and countersuits had given way to an ultimatum. Hodges had agreed to resign as chairman unless he could find a buyer for the bank at twenty-three dollars a share or better by December 31, 1989. It was March. Nine months to pull it off.

As we became reacquainted, Luther and I shared steak, Scotch, and cigars. It seems that many of the people I liked best came with these sinful vices. But it was his *political* story that won my allegiance.

Albeit a Democrat, Luther Hodges was a kindred spirit, a political junkie like me. But he was on the politician side; I was on the behind-the-scenes side. The son of a famous father, Luther ran for the senate in North Carolina, and lost. While his father had been secretary of commerce for John F. Kennedy, Luther was deputy commerce secretary for Jimmy Carter. I could sense in Luther a sort of falling short feeling. But more recently, he could almost feel the golden ring touch his hand. He became the national finance chairman for a dream candidate, an almost certain presidential winner. It all turned to ashes over a single weekend when Gary Hart was photographed with Donna Rice.

Having endured Gerald Ford's close loss, I could feel his pain. We were brothers-in-arms.

So I accepted Luther's invitation to stand shoulder to shoulder with him to fend off the Arabs. I became a senior vice president of the National Bank of Washington and together we threw ourselves into finding a buyer for the bank. Without asking, Luther wrote me a contract that provided if he was no longer chairman of the board on January first, I would have the option to leave with a year's severance. Perhaps he was the only one thinking ahead.

I also worked closely with the bank's chief operating officer, Bill Wooten, to keep the employees focused while NBW was ravaged in the press everyday. I had the financial reporter from *The Washington Post* on speed dial, and I spent many evenings with her dishing background color.

We came tantalizingly close. We had competing offers just below twenty dollars a share. But, as the deadline approached, we could not nudge them over the line. Luther resigned, as he promised. The game was over.

Bill Wooten asked me to stay. "We'll need you more than ever," he said. He offered me a contract with a year's severance for a "termination," or "constructive termination" of my services. I felt I was covered for any outcome. But Luther was the reason I was there, and without Luther, my heart wasn't in a position at the bank.

I told Bill Wooten I would exercise my exit under Luther's contract, but I would stay for a month or two at no salary to help out. He shook my hand with gratitude.

The third day into my free service, Luther hosted a "steak and whiskey" farewell dinner at his favorite Washington club. Most of the NBW senior officers were present, and it became a long night of camaraderie and reminisces. The soiree was covered sympathetically in *The Washington Post* the next day.

Bill Wooten came to my office with a long face. "You won't need to come in anymore," he said. "Luther loyalists are no longer in favor with the new board."

Kicked out of my pro bono job. At the new White House I had an "R" (for Reagan) after my name. At the new NBW, I had an "H" (for Hodges). I had no regrets on either front.

The Arabs failed miserably in running the bank. In four months, employees were called into the conference room to be told the FDIC was seizing the bank. "If you have any contracts, they are null and void. If you have accrued vacation time, it is cancelled. Your employee benefits cease as of twelve noon today. You should go back to your desk, gather your personal items, and take them to the door to be inspected. Your services are terminated." My erstwhile contract protection would have been useless.

Your government in action.

\* \* \*

Luther Hodges moved to Santa Fe, New Mexico, and started the popular magazine *The Santa Fean*. We still visit each other in retirement and rail about the barbarians at the gate. The NBW

Headquarters building at 14th and H Street in Washington, on the National Register of Historic Places, has been vacant for two decades. Long-planned attempts to turn it into the American Genocide Museum are ongoing.

On the first anniversary, we held a raucous reunion of the *Hailstone* rescue team at an Italian restaurant where the spouses heard more about sailing than they ever cared to know. The "hurricane" we braved was even more fearsome in retrospect. *Hailstone* was now safely berthed on "J" Dock at the Gangplank Marina in Washington, D.C.

# THE RONALD REAGAN
# PRESIDENTIAL LIBRARY

Considering the haphazard attention I have given to my employment, I enjoyed another stroke of good fortune when Ron Kaufman (bless him) circulated my name for a variety of sub-cabinet positions in the Bush administration. Ron told me he needed some gray beards with actual experience. For once my advanced age was an advantage.

Only a month after NBW went dark, I received a call from Jim Kolstad, chairman of the National Transportation Safety Board. He wanted to interview me to become the managing director of the agency (chief operating officer).

It was another serendipitous fit. Jim Kolstad had been an advanceman in the Nixon years. He, like me, considered an advanceman Superman in civilian clothes. After talking about NTSB, we started relating tales from the road that lasted well into the afternoon. It was a comfortable match. We clicked, and shook hands on the job.

NTSB must be one of the best jobs in government. An independent agency of the United States government, NTSB is the CSI of accident investigation—principally airplane crash investigations, but all modes of transportation come under NTSB's purview, so rail, marine, pipeline, and highway incidents of spectacular magnitude are investigated. Employees possessed high esprit de corps—two hundred fifty aerospace engineers and accident experts who were the best in the world at what they do, and knew it. NTSB regularly confronted front-page incidents, which turned into the mystery of the week for us to unravel. The assignment was exhilarating.

But I also encountered the maddening bureaucracy of a government agency for the first time—unending political maneuvering between the members of the board; lax budget controls; employees who had retired on the job, yet could not be dislodged; mind-numbing purchase regulations, which made federal equipment more expensive than the same items for business, and on and on. One by one, we confronted what we could, and lived with what we couldn't. *Maintain an even strain.* Churchill might have been restless, but Harris would have been proud. All things considered, it was a wonderful four years. I took a short leave in 1991 to do the dedication celebration of the Ronald Reagan Presidential Library near Los Angeles, California. Another chance to work with Jim Hooley, Mike Deaver, Andrew Littlefair, Shelby Scarbrough, and a host of other old friends.

The library is spectacular, sitting high on a hill in Simi Valley, with a view all the way to the Pacific. About four thousand VIPs and guests were expected for the grand opening. The outdoor event would feature a Blue Angel flyover and the first ever gathering of five United States presidents in one place.

Six first ladies also attended. Other celebrity guests included Bob Hope and Jimmy Stewart, and Caroline and John Kennedy, Jr., who were gracious participants. One of my personal highpoints was to finally meet Ashley Parker's father.

We rehearsed all the movements of the principals with various members of our team acting as stand-ins for the presidents and first ladies. I had the role of Gerald Ford, perhaps in recognition of my receding hairline. My photo of the "first family impersonators" is another prized memento.

Reagan weather prevailed on the day of the ceremony; it was sunny and warm. Hot, in fact. After the speeches, the five presidents were to walk together into the library, but John Sununu, George Bush's chief of staff, inserted himself in the middle of the five, arms ostentatiously over their shoulders, to ruin the historic photo.

On the way through the courtyard, Pat Nixon became dizzy, apparently overcome by the long sun exposure. President Nixon guided her to a bench halfway to the library entrance, where they were immediately engulfed by well-wishers from the departing audience. I could see Nixon's look of distress. Ron Walker, his long-time aide, also came to their assistance. Ron and I urged the crowd to step back to give the couple air, but autograph seekers began to push forward like over-eager children with a new puppy. To say I was disgusted barely describes it.

Nixon suddenly stood and led his wobbling wife toward the door while Ron and I ran interference. Inside, they both looked shaky, so Ron took them directly to the car rather than the reception.

While the VIPs mingled, the guests toured the library for the first time. (It is well worth a trip to Simi Valley.) At the conclusion of the luncheon, President and Mrs. Reagan circled the room to thank each of us for our assistance over the years. It would be the last time I saw the president in person.

* * *

Back at NTSB, the accidents were both tragic and fascinating. Some images stayed forever: the *Exxon Valdez* in a massive dry dock, her bottom completely pulverized; the could-not-make-it-up encounter of the *Houston* and *Barcona*—a US Navy nuclear sub on a movie shoot, snagging the towline between a tug and barge, and pulling the tug under and killing three crewmen; and the incredible story of United Flight 232.

United 232 was a DC-10 en route from Denver to Chicago when the tail mounted engine blew up. The DC-10 also has two under-wing engines, so at first the incident was only a blip. But within moments, the flight crew noticed the hydraulic pressure was falling. Hydraulics powered all of the flight controls. There were three redundant systems, but all ran through the tail section where engine shrapnel had severed the lines. The pilots helplessly watched as all three systems went dead.

After several futile moments of trying flaps, ailerons, and rudder controls with no success, captain Al Haynes slumped in his seat and said, "Guys, we're not going to make it to the ground."

A long thirty seconds of silence followed. Haynes sat forward again. The only controls left were the throttles. Haynes started experimenting with differential throttle inputs and found he could crudely steer the plane this way.

In a series of looping turns, United 232 diverted to Sioux City, Iowa, where Haynes, defying all expectations, actually got the aircraft lined up for the runway. But with no flaps to slow the plane, and no fine control to adjust the wing levels, a landing was too much to hope for. A wing tip touched and the plane went out of control, breaking apart and catching fire. A hundred and twelve people died in the crash, but a hundred and eighty-five lived, including Al Haynes.

There was an extensive NTSB investigation, with an interesting debate about the cause of the engine failure. But the bigger story was the miraculous skill of Captain Haynes. NTSB loaded data from the United 232 black boxes into a flight simulator. Some of the most experienced pilots in America tried their hand at flying the simulator to Sioux City and landing.

No one got as close as Al Haynes.

The dramatic incident has served as the starting point for several recent movie plots.

* * *

My last advance was at my request. I read that Vice President Dan Quayle was to be the grand marshal for the Indianapolis 500, one of my favorite annual sporting events. I called friends in the vice president's Advance Office to find out if I could do the trip to the 500. Yes, but I would have to lead another

Quayle trip first, to earn my spurs. More vacation days from NTSB.

While my impressions of Dan Quayle were less than gold-plated, they were all second-hand—watching his disastrous introduction as a candidate followed by an equally disastrous debate with Lloyd Bentsen and hearing about Joe Canzeri's travails as his campaign aide. I was hoping that time in his role as vice president had tempered him and I was looking forward to liking him.

My optimism was misplaced.

My earn-the-spurs event was a fundraising dinner in Texas. It was the last stop of a several-day Quayle swing out west. The host committee was a delightful group, easy to work with. I liked them all. So, I was personally embarrassed when Vice President Quayle arrived an hour and a half early and rejected the obvious suggestion that he hold on the plane or take some private time in the room we had arranged.

No, Quayle was eager to return to Washington. No waiting around. He made one lap of the dinner site with his entourage, greeting the workers, still decorating. A few early arrivals earned a brief handshake.

Fully an hour before the reception was scheduled to begin, Quayle departed.

The patrons who had paid to dine with him, who might have hoped for some uplifting comments to share with their friends, arrived to find a reception in disarray and disappointment turning to anger. Oh, but they each received a machine-signed Dan Quayle photograph.

My friend in the vice president's Advance Office had my sympathy, and my immediate withdrawal from the Indy 500 event.

* * *

As the first term of George H. W. Bush wound down, I called Ron Kaufman to urge him to begin to rotate advancemen to the White House staff where they could start to prepare political events.

"Have you seen our numbers?" Ron asked. "We have a 90 percent approval rating. We won't even need a campaign."

It was a miscalculation that failed to anticipate the challenge of Ross Perot or the talents of Bill Clinton. Bush's numbers plunged as the economy slowed.


Back at NTSB, we confronted vexing issues big and small.

Big: I purchased our two hundred new computers at Circuit City, where the price was dramatically lower than the GSA (General Services Administration) schedule (the price government agencies were to pay to the GSA for equipment and supplies). I thought it would be idiotic to pay substantially more to the GSA instead of walking down the street to get a bargain. Our two hundred computers outside the system created a significant savings for the taxpayers.

GSA told me I had committed a felony by ignoring their purchasing rules; they were planning to prosecute me. I told them I would be pleased to defend my decision at a

Congressional hearing to air the issue. I never heard anything more. Hopefully the statute of limitations has run out.

Small: the grandly named "Interagency Task Force on Government Smoking" asked me to host a meeting in my office. I had a conflicting meeting, so I asked my deputy, Lloyd, a career government employee and a good one, to fill in. I returned three hours later to find the meeting still underway behind closed doors.

While my loyal secretary, Pearl, tried to contain her giggles, I pulled out a gigantic Churchill cigar and fired it up. I popped into the room, pausing, as if surprised. "Oh, Lloyd. You are still meeting." I blew out a huge cloud of cigar smoke. "Sorry." I stepped back out and closed the door.

There was a stunned moment of silence. Pearl pressed her hands across her mouth. Then a loud burst of laughter as the Interagency Task Force on Government Smoking realized they had been spoofed. "That was our managing director," Lloyd said with his hands outstretched as if to say, *See what we have to contend with from these political appointees.*


Times were changing. Jim Kolstad's five-year term as NTSB board member ended in 1992. President Bush nominated Carl Vogt, a distinguished lawyer with Fulbright Jaworski, to become the new chairman. Jim and Carl were both superb colleagues and continue to be friends. They helped make government service important and effective. I was proud to serve with both of them.

Needless to say, the biggest change was still to come. George Bush lost the presidency to Bill Clinton in November 1992.

Ross Perot syphoned off 19 percent of the popular vote. Clinton won 32 states and 370 electoral votes.

I served "at the pleasure of the president," so after Clinton's inauguration, I was expecting the call. Carl Vogt urged me to just keep on doing what I was doing. "We need you," he said. It seems to be a claim I can't resist.

It wasn't until March 1993 that the Clinton White House got around to thinking about NTSB. The call came from a newly minted White House staffer who sounded like she was a teenager. "When do you intend to resign?" she asked, with no preamble.

"Do you have a new managing director ready to send over?" I replied.

"That is really not your concern," she said.

"It really *is* my concern," I said. "I have no intention of resigning until someone is ready to take over the agency. I care about NTSB."

She sounded befuddled. Calls from the White House were supposed to be answered with deference. "I'll get back to you," she mumbled.

The next call came in May, from an older, more prepossessed woman. "I want your resignation on my desk by the end of the week."

"I'll be happy to submit a letter when I've had a chance to brief your candidate for the job."

She sputtered. "That's not the way it works."

"It's the way it works for me," I said.

She hung up.

Another month passed. The call from the heavy-hitter came in June—the director of White House personnel. "Let's cut to the chase," he said, the reasonable businessman. "If he wanted to, the president could reappoint the entire Safety Board as he sees fit."

"Well, not actually," I said, annoyed that he didn't seem to understand the board members served for fixed terms. Of course that did not apply to me, but why do his homework for him. I decided on misdirection. "Have you read the Independent Safety Act of 1966?" I asked.

After a long pause, he said, "No."

"Why don't you study it and get back to me."

I had just made it up.

I imagined interns combing the records in vain for the Independent Safety Act of 1966. But I began to pack up my desk. I was ready to leave, but I really did want a capable replacement to manage the staff.

In the end, another stroke of the luck that had characterized my career intervened. Jack Byrne sold Fireman's Fund Insurance Company to Alliance of Germany. He retained the holding company, the public shareholders, and the three billion dollar investment portfolio as partial payment for the insurance company operations. He called to say he thought two or three people could manage the runoff of the portfolio over several years and return the proceeds to shareholders. We would be a "melting ice-cube." At the end of our mission, we would dust off our hands and become country squires. He wanted to end his career with his favorite people in his favorite place, Hanover,

New Hampshire, home of Dartmouth College. Would I come to New England to help him?

*Would I.* It was manna from heaven.

I made my farewells at NTSB and moved to New Hampshire in July.

It took the Clinton administration nearly a year to confirm a new managing director for NTSB.

\* \* \*

After leaving the White House, Mike Deaver formed his own public relations firm, Michael K. Deaver, Inc., and later was chairman of Edelman Public Relations. He died in 2007. When the author of one puff piece claimed that Deaver's public relations skills had "made" Ronald Reagan, Deaver replied, "No, Ronald Reagan made me."

Jim Kolstad became the chief safety expert for the American Automobile Association, and later, the executive director of the Chemical Manufacturers' Association. Jim inspects my boat once or twice a year.

Carl Vogt left NTSB at the end of his term to return to Fulbright Jaworski. He served as president of his alma mater, Williams College, in 1999. In 2006, the National Aeronautic Association, the oldest aviation association in the United States, named him an "Elder Statesman of Aviation." I look forward to being old enough for this honor.

Ron Kaufman formed his own consulting firm in Washington, where he remains one of the most influential and connected powerbrokers in the nation.

Jack Byrne, my role model and mentor for thirty years, was inducted into the International Insurance Hall of Fame in 2009. The holding company we moved to New Hampshire in 1993 to become a "melting ice-cube" has instead become a major financial services enterprise named The White Mountains Insurance Group, now ably led by Ray Barrette.

In the twenty years since I left NTSB, I have often followed the agency's accomplishments with pride, and remember the many outstanding employees with affection.

# Personal Glimpses

After so many Novembers spent on campaigns, it was a surprise to wake up one morning and find myself in the November of my years. I couldn't count the sets of shoes I've worn out crisscrossing event sites, but the ache in my knees is a constant reminder. Perhaps the bionic energy is beginning to ebb.

Recounting some of these stories has brought a parade of faces and names back into focus. I've had incredible luck in my career, but even more good fortune in working with a life-long group of memorable people: Mark Hatfield, Joe Canzeri, Steve Studdert, Jim Hooley, Jim Kolstad, Carl Vogt, Luther Hodges, Jr., Bill Harris, Chris Ambrose, Jim Miller, Ron Kaufman, Ray Barrette, and Jack Byrne, to name a few. Bill Henkel delivered in full on his promise that I would make lifelong friendships.

As I am writing these lines, Jack Byrne has just died after a long illness. For thirty-five years, Jack was a central fixture of my life. Mentor, boss, Rock of Gibraltar. He was the gravitational pull about which we orbited, honored to be part of a happy solar system. We almost wonder how we can go on when he, at long last, has been able to rest. The answer is, *that* is why he led us, challenged us, taught us, and pushed us. That is what he would expect of us.

Jack would often say, "You're in charge," then add with a twinkle, "Just don't screw up."

We will try our best, Jack.

I feel the same appreciation for Ronald Reagan. He was an inspirational president. We were honored with the opportunity to be part of a great experience and leave with treasured memories.

$$* \; * \; *$$

One of the special privileges of working with great men is the chance to know the man behind the mask. Small, private backstage moments offer an insight into character and personality unscripted by speechwriters or filtered by the press. Often these behind-the-scenes encounters flash by with little notice, yet bubble up later to bring a smile at the memory. Here are a few of those personal glimpses.

## CANZERI

Part of Joe Canzeri's appeal was that he was comfortable with himself. He knew who he was. Unlike so many of the political animals around him, he had nothing to prove. He was never afraid to poke fun at himself.

Joe Canzeri's short stature was frequently grist for the mill. When he showed me his favorite photo with Presidents Reagan, Nixon, Ford, and Carter, whom Joe accompanied to Sadat's funeral, he noted that the man in the middle (himself) should have "stood on a box."

Mike Deaver sometimes called Joe his "Latin Leprechaun." When Deaver returned from the scene of Reagan's near-assassination, where Deaver threw himself to the ground as the bullet whizzed by, he said to Joe, "You would have been safe. You wouldn't even have to duck."

Hugh Morrow, a colleague from Rockefeller's team, said, "Canzeri has the tactical skills and resourcefulness of Napoleon—he's also the same approximate size."

When Joe Canzeri's son, Stuart, made up a list of questions for the president on behalf of his sixth-grade class, Joe dutifully approached Reagan with a tape recorder and the president answered each question. Afterwards, Joe discovered he had pressed the wrong button. The tape was blank.

Reagan patiently did it all over.

## BACKSTAGE HUMOR

One of the elevators in the United States Mission to the United Nations is so small that even conforming to the manifest, we were crammed together. The fellow sardines were President Reagan, four Secret Service agents, and me. As the doors closed, Reagan, elbow-to-elbow with all of us, looked around at the agents and said to me, "Do you think we'll be safe enough in this elevator?"

The lead agent immediately deadpanned, "I'm not sure. How much money have you got on you?"

## THE MONSTER

President Reagan had a guttural vocalization sometimes noticeable between his sentences, a sort of heavy rasping that was more pronounced when he was tired. We called it "the monster," as in "the monster is out this afternoon, we have to get the president some rest." It was not a comment of mockery, but of care.

After all the years, we were each developing our own monsters.

## A NIXON KEEPSAKE

Secret Service agent Ed Russell told me about protecting Richard Nixon after he left the White House. Unlike Ronald Reagan, who knew every agent by name, Nixon just addressed them generically, as "agent."

Nixon's memoir had just come out, and his team of agents each bought a copy. Russell and agent George Godlesky brought the armloads of books to Nixon to request autographs. Each book had the agent's name taped on the front, and a slip inside to indicate to whom the inscription should be written. For instance, Godlesky's book was intended for his mother. Nixon agreeably took the books into his office.

When Nixon came back out, he handed the books to Russell and Godlesky. "Agent," Nixon said, "I fucked this first one up. I signed the inscription to agent Godlesky before I noticed he wanted it to be for his mother. I wrote another inscription to his mother on the next page. So, here is what you do. Take a razor blade and cut the first page out. This guy Godlesky will never be the wiser." Russell and Godlesky winked conspiratorially.

George Godlesky chuckled to himself and saved both pages. He is the only agent who will have Nixon's memoir with two inscriptions.

## NORMANDY BEACHES

One of the more memorable presidential days was the Fortieth Anniversary of the Invasion of Normandy when Ronald Reagan stopped at each of the five D-Day beaches. It was enough to give even non-believers the faith that someone was smiling on the president. As the motorcade arrived at the first beach, the rain stopped and the sun came out. President Reagan made his remarks and returned to the motorcade. As the doors closed, the rain began again. At the next beach, the rain stopped and the sun came out. This happened as if on divine cue at each of the beaches. Rain, sun, rain, sun.

Then the motorcade headed to the American Cemetery for a small ceremony in the chapel. After the Secret Service sweep earlier in the day, the agent locked the door to the chapel. In the normal course of events, the agent rotated down the hill to the next post. As he saw the motorcade approaching, the agent suddenly realized he still had the key and sprinted up the hill.

The motorcade stopped and waited. All the staff with radio earpieces knew what was causing the delay, but the president was in the dark. He looked curiously out each window and finally asked his agent, "Why are we waiting?"

His agent confessed with chagrin, "Well, sir, we seem to have misplaced the key to the chapel."

"Ah," the president said bemused, "maybe the Jackal has it."

## REMEMBERING A PRESIDENT

In 1994, Ronald Reagan told the world in a handwritten note that he had been diagnosed with Alzheimer's disease. He wrote, "I now begin the journey that will lead me into the sunset of my life." Admirers from around the world sent him messages of encouragement and love. Mrs. Reagan and the library staff kept us informed. We were all moved.

In 1999, I attended a White House staff reunion at the Reagan Library in California to celebrate President Reagan's eighty-eighth birthday. Merv Griffin and William F. Buckley hosted a dinner party for the occasion. But while Reagan had been regularly visiting his office in Century City up to a few weeks before, it soon became obvious from the false starts and Nancy Reagan's anxious watch-checking that the president was not in any condition to attend the party. It was a pleasant but sad reunion.

Ronald Reagan died on June 5, 2004. President Bush declared a National Day of Mourning. Rick Ahearn and our old pals from the Military District of Washington arranged the State Funeral at the Washington National Cathedral. Reagan's body was then flown to Point Mugu, the Naval Air Station where he had landed many times to visit his ranch in Santa Barbara.

Fittingly, Jim Hooley presided over the California events, which included the slow trip from Point Mugu to Simi Valley, where the streets and overpasses were filled with mourners, reminiscent of the slow pass of the *Heartland Express* through the farms of central Ohio in 1984.

Ronald Reagan was laid to rest at the Reagan Library, overlooking the Pacific Ocean. Mikhail Gorbachev was there to give Ronald Reagan's coffin a pat. Jim Hooley and several others who had advanced the ceremony waited on the balcony of the Reagan Library until all the guests had left, then, well after midnight, assisted the agent rolling the casket into the crypt.

Jim Hooley, Mike Lake, Andrew Littlefair, and Gary Foster each scattered a handful of earth on the casket.

"We took him home," Jim said with a hitch in his voice.

## MARK HATFIELD

Mark Hatfield and I have continued to share memories over steak and whiskey. Mark is the master of the colorful phrase. He recalls events with the same enthusiasm he experienced while living them. With the perspective of several decades, one night Mark summarized what it all meant to him:

"The incredibly tense and meaningful experiences we had gave me a wonderful freedom from ever feeling I hadn't done enough in my life. I read somewhere there is no such thing as a mid-life crisis, only an all-life crisis, which has finally been recognized. I think I will skip the crisis. I saw so much, did so much, went to so many places, it's given me the freedom to focus on things that may seem more subdued, or mundane, or tame, but are part of life's mix that bring fulfillment. I'll never worry I missed anything. Now I have the freedom to focus on quieter chapters.

"It may seem indirect. It may be a byproduct, but I think it's the most important thing I got. I proved it, I did it, I experienced it. I was there when history was made.

"That's not to ignore that I gained life skills over the years of advance work—confidence, communications skills, templates I can put over anything. Nothing is impossible, look beyond boundaries, think outside the box. I gained the 'done' ethic (Canzeri would smile). I learned to take responsibility from the

Walkers, and Studderts, and Canzeris who demanded results not excuses. God, it was great, wasn't it?"

Mark's words helped me understand why Joe Canzeri was so comfortable in his skin, and helped me appreciate why I was too.

Of course, the purpose of our campaign events had been to create energy and support for a presidential election. We worked hard and played hard. But my happiest memories are of those times our buoyant crowds and special touches lifted the spirits of the president after a difficult debate or exhausting summit trip.

Mere advancemen had done it.

# Acknowledgments

Appreciation goes to my first readers, Stanley and Karen Hubbard, and Drew and Penny Cunningham. Their insights and encouragement were priceless.

My advance colleagues Mark Rosenker, Joe Canzeri, Mark Hatfield, and especially Jim Hooley were generous with their time and their stories. I appropriated some of their tales for *November's Gladiators,* but they retained a treasure trove of memories for their own books, which will be "must-reads."

Thanks to my agent of thirty years, Audrey Wolf, who only had to wait twenty-five years for this third manuscript.

And gratitude to the team at Langdon Street Press, particularly Kate Ankofski, editorial director, and my editor Jennifer Gehlhar, as well as Allison, Ashley, Sophie, and Kevin, who made the publishing process a pleasure.

# About the Author

Terry Baxter is the author of two acclaimed suspense novels, *Hailstone* and *The Ursa Ultimatum*. He spent time as a television director, race car driver, Hollywood stunt man, and a senior executive in business and the federal government. He divides his time between New Hampshire and Key Largo, Florida. Please visit his website at: www.NOVEMBERSGLADIATORS.com.